SEMANTICS

IN THE SAME SERIES

Editor: Richard Hudson

SEMANTICS

Howard Gregory

London and New York

First published 2000
by Routledge
11 New Fetter Lane, London EC4P 4EE

Simultaneously published in the USA and Canada
by Routledge
29 West 35th Street, New York, NY 10001

Routledge is an imprint of the Taylor & Francis Group

Typeset in Times Ten by Florence Production Ltd,
Stoodleigh, Devon

Printed and bound in Great Britain by
TJ International Ltd, Padstow, Cornwall

British Library Cataloguing in Publication Data
A catalogue record for this book is available from the British Library

Library of Congress Cataloging in Publication Data
Gregory, Howard, 1960–
   Semantics : an introductory workbook / Howard Gregory.
     p.   cm. — (Language workbooks)
   Includes bibliographical references and index.
   ISBN 0-415-21610-9 (pbk.)
   1. Semantics.   I. Title. II. Series.
   P325.G685 2000
   401'.43—dc21
                                           99–39900
                                                CIP

ISBN 0–415–21610–9

To the people of Romania

CONTENTS

USING THIS BOOK

This book is intended to meet the need for a genuinely introductory course book in semantics. It is intended for undergraduates, probably beginning a linguistics-related course, who find themselves having to deal with semantics for the first time. It is quite common for such students to start off by being confused and discouraged, primarily perhaps because it is not always easy to appreciate the relevance of semantic approaches, which can appear very abstract, to their own interests in language. This book starts from very simple observations about meaning, and gradually shows how meanings are built up and inter-related. It presupposes very little prior knowledge either of grammar or of linguistic terminology. (Technical terms introduced in the book are distinguished by small capitals, and are listed in a Glossary at the end.)

Unlike many books in this field it is *not* intended as a textbook in logic, though you will pick up a certain amount of logic in the course of working through it. The emphasis is on analysing the meaning of basic expressions of natural (i.e. human) language. Logic comes into it because it has been found a useful tool for doing this – at least in one of the most influential traditions within linguistics, one which is strongly reflected here. Of course for serious work in semantics a more detailed knowledge of logic is needed than can be given here.

This is designed to be used as a *course* book (rather than a traditional textbook), and you will get the most out of it if you work through the exercises. Most of these have answers at the back, which you are advised to check, as they may be picked up in later work.

Some ideas from set theory are used during the book – these are quite intuitive and non-technical, but there is a short appendix on sets and functions (section 10.1).

Thanks are due first of all to my first teachers of semantics, Shalom Lappin and Ruth Kempson. I am also indebted to Dick Hudson, whose unerring advice made this a better book than I would have written unaided; and to several anonymous readers. Finally I would like to thank Louisa Semlyen, Miranda Filbee and Katharine Jacobson for supporting the book and seeing it through into print.

PINNING DOWN SEMANTICS

1

Semantics is 'the study of meaning'. For the purposes of this book, the object of study is the meaning of human language (sometimes termed 'natural language'). It should not be forgotten, of course, that other structured systems (programming languages, diagrams, rituals, mathematical formulas) all have an appropriate concept of meaning, and hence their own semantics.

So what is meaning? Well, at one level 'meaning' is an ordinary English word, which like most words can be used in a number of different ways. Some of them are illustrated by the sentences in (1.1).

1.1 How else could you describe each of these uses of the word 'mean'?

    a   It's a good job he doesn't know what 'malaka' means.
    b   I'm sure she didn't mean to pour olive oil in your hair.
    c   Mean it? I didn't even *say* it.
    d   I think that means she isn't coming back.
    e   So he's Russian. Does that mean he's good at chess?
    f   'Irony is the gap between what is said and what is meant'.

But semantics is not about the use of a particular English word, or its correlates in other languages, though these may give us clues about the area under discussion. The Greek word (from which we get 'semantics') conveys the idea of *importance* (compare the English words 'meaningful' or 'significant'). The Chinese equivalent is also used to mean *interest*. This suggests that the subject touches on questions of why people bother to use language in the first place, and why we bother to listen to them. It is certainly a far cry from what people have in mind when they dismiss something as 'a matter of semantics'!

However, semantics as covered by this book is more limited in scope. In terms of the contrast in sentence f above, it is confined largely to the study of 'what is said', leaving aside such interesting issues as irony, metaphor, and social interaction. It tries to characterize the meaning of expressions in relation to other expressions, and in relation to the objects and situations about which they offer information.

1.1
FORM AND
CONTENT

Take a simple word like 'book'. It can be analysed at many different levels. First of all we know how it is pronounced and spelt (or spelled?); this is one kind of information. And when we encounter it, we associate it in some way with *books* – either some mental concept of them, or objects in the real world instantiating the concept (never mind which for the moment). The first thing is to distinguish systematically between the first kind of information, which concerns 'book' as an expression in a language, and the second kind, which we can call (very provisionally) the concept of *book*. Typographically, this distinction will be re-inforced by using quotation marks for the former and italics for the latter, as in the previous sentence. (A word of warning: many linguistics books use different conventions.)

It may help to think of situations where words in different languages are said to 'mean the same thing'. For example, 'book', 'livre', 'carte' 'kniga' and 'hon' are expressions in different languages, but are associated with the same concept, *book*. Note that although I have used an English word to label the concept, this is just a matter of convenience. I could have used anything – a word in another language, a number, or a little picture of a book. Equally, I am not implying that speakers of all languages have exactly the same stock of concepts.

Conversely a single word may have more than one meaning. For example the English word 'table' can mean an item of furniture or a kind of chart. To avoid confusing the two meanings (not likely in this case, but it is not always so simple), we should use different labels for the two concepts. Since these labels are arbitrary anyway, one way of doing it is to use *table*$_1$ and *table*$_2$ respectively (rather like in a dictionary). These may be termed word senses, as opposed to word forms.

There is no guarantee that a single word form in another language will cover the same group of word senses. For example in Greek 'trapezi' means what I have called *table*$_1$, while to express *table*$_2$ you would have to use a different word form, like 'pinakas'. However, certain clusters of word senses often go together in many languages.

EXERCISES

synonyms

1.2   If two word forms share at least one word sense, then they are SYNONYMS. Pick out synonyms from the following list, and make sentences illustrating the word sense which they share (note that some of these senses may be specific to colloquial British English). The words may have slightly different connotations – it is quite rare to find *exact* synonyms in language.

store	lies	gift	bottle	porkies	current
guts	shop	hoard	intestines	present	betray

1.3 Conversely if two distinct word senses correspond to one word form, they are known as HOMONYMS. The 'same word form' can of course be defined in terms of sound or spelling, depending which medium is being used. (In the first case they are called 'homophones', in the second case 'homographs' – two different types of homonym.) Make pairs of homonyms of either kind based on the words below.

homonyms

drag	wrap	wheel	read	polish	practice

1.4 Investigate whether English word forms with more than one sense correspond to the same word form in some other language known to you; and compare results. (You may be able to do this using a good bilingual dictionary.) Here are a few to start you off:

head	branch	cheek	sex	hard	appointment
black	field	terribly	way	bird	board
miss	pass				

One simple approach to meaning is to associate each expression with a particular object in the world. This seems more or less plausible with certain types of expression, such as proper names: 'Bill Clinton' or 'Saddam Hussein', for example seem to refer to recognizable individuals. Similarly phrases like 'the Eiffel Tower' or 'the moon' seem to pick out particular objects. This idea of picking out objects can be termed the REFERENCE of an expression (the object picked out is its REFERENT).

1.2 OBJECTS AND THEIR DESCRIPTIONS

reference
referent

✐ **EXERCISE**

1.5 List the words and phrases in this text which have the same referent.

> Einstein College today announced the firing of its director. The chairman of the board of governors said that he had phoned him last night to inform him that his services were no longer required. This follows overspending on a new residence for students, with resulting cutbacks in academic programs. Their representative, Tracy Sharpe, commented that they now had nice accommodation but no professors.

Reference appears to be an important part of meaning. For example, words like 'it' and 'they', which occur in some form in all languages, depend on it. But it is easy to see that this cannot be the whole story.

EXERCISE

1.6 What are the referents of the following expressions? (i) 'the president of the USA'; (ii) 'the World Cup winners'; (iii) 'the highest mountain in the world'; (iv) 'the first astronaut'.

These are easy enough to answer, but the problem with this exercise (or pseudo-exercise) is that it reads like part of a trivia quiz, rather than an analysis of meaning. It is possible to be mistaken about the answer to one of these questions (i.e. the referent of the phrase) while understanding perfectly its meaning (in the intuitive sense). Moreover the referent of some of these descriptions changes with time. As I write this chapter, the referent of the first is Bill Clinton (or let's say *bill_clinton*, the same object that is the referent of 'Bill Clinton'). But this may well not be the case by the time it goes into print. On the other hand we would hardly want to say that 'the president of the USA' has changed its meaning.

There are other considerations as well. To take a well-known example, 'the morning star' and 'the evening star' refer to the same object. But it would seem paradoxical to say that they have the same meaning, especially given that 'morning' and 'evening' have (intuitively) opposite meanings. Again, if they had the same meaning, then the discovery that the two phenomena are one planet would hardly be news. It would be like discovering that $1 = 1$. And so with all factual discoveries about the identity of objects.

Thus reference cannot be the whole of meaning. What I have called the 'intuitive sense' of meaning, which remains constant when the referent changes, is often called the SENSE of an expression. If we know its sense, we should be able to pick out its referent in any particular set of circumstances, as long as we know the appropriate facts.

sense

I am going to introduce another terminological distinction, that between reference and DENOTATION (though you should note that sometimes these are used almost interchangeably). If I use the phrase 'the queen', I am likely to be referring to *queen_elizabeth_II*, the daughter of *george_VI* and the mother of *prince_charles*. On such occasions, she will be the referent of the phrase. But its denotation is something more abstract. It will include all those individuals that could be referred to using the word 'queen'. If you like, it is classifying objects into those which come under the heading 'queen' and those which don't. More precisely, it includes those entities which can be classified by a given sense of the word 'queen'. If you see a pub called 'The Queen's Head' with a picture of Freddie Mercury

denotation

outside it, a different word sense and hence a different scheme of classification is at work.

──

✎ **EXERCISE**

1.7 For each of these words, distinguish at least two senses. Give two examples of individuals or objects which fall within the denotation of each word sense, and give an example sentence in which they are the intended referent.

    a   bank
    b   star
    c   pig

──

1.3 CONTENT AND CONTEXT

The distinction between denotation and reference brings into focus another crucial aspect of meaning – the context in which an expression is used. To take an obvious example, the phrase 'my wife' can be used by any number of men, normally referring to a different woman in each case. Likewise the referent of 'yesterday's paper' depends when the expression is used (besides the speaker and his or her reading habits). We have to account for the fact that the same expression used in different contexts may have the same meaning in some respects but different in other respects, notably reference.

It is helpful here to distinguish between TOKEN and TYPE. To take some standard non-linguistic examples, two pound coins are two different objects but they are instances of 'the same thing'. They are two tokens of one type of object. Similarly the 10 a.m. flight to Bucharest is 'the same flight' each day, though the actual aircraft used may be different. (The relevant criteria of sameness or difference depend, of course, on the level of detail required.)

token
type

──

✎ **EXERCISE**

1.8 Count the words in the last sentence, first the number of word tokens and then the number of word types.

──

In language, the same expression, say a sentence, may be used on different occasions. It is 'the same', that is, as far as its phonological and syntactic analysis is concerned, but used at different times or by different speakers (and showing small phonetic variations which may be irrelevant to its linguistics structure). It can be said that it is the same sentence but different utterances of that sentence. The terminology I will adopt here is to say that it comprises one sentence type but several sentence tokens. A token occurs in a context, and this context will normally affect its meaning; especially its reference and that of its subparts.

EXERCISE ✎

1.9 How many sentence types and tokens are there in this exchange?

    a   'My theory of X-bar syntax is better than yours.'
    b   'No it isn't. My theory of X-bar syntax is better than yours.'
    a   'Look, it's simple. I'm right and you're wrong.'
    b   'Don't be so childish. I'm right and you're wrong.'

How does the reference change between different tokens of the same sentence type?

As has already been hinted, linguistics in general is more concerned with utterance types than tokens. Suppose in a given situation Mary says to you, 'My computer's crashed.' You can get different kinds of information – that she is still alive, that she speaks English (perhaps with an accent which tells you where she comes from), that she is still talking to you – but linguistic semantics concerns itself with the information offered about her computer. That is derived from the sentence type, in conjunction with *some* contextual information, namely that which identifies the speaker as Mary. The branch of study that concerns itself more extensively with the interpretation of utterances in context is known as PRAGMATICS. This is the subject of another book in this series, written by Jean Peccei. The exact borderline between semantics and pragmatics is a hazy one, but the relationship between them is certainly a very close one. This must be the case because for many linguistic expressions a crucial part of their meaning (including reference, and hence the truth or falsity of sentences) cannot be determined without looking at context.

pragmatics

1.4
WORDS AND SENTENCES

lexical semantics

truth-conditional semantics

There are two main approaches to linguistic semantics. The first, LEXICAL SEMANTICS, focuses on the meaning of words. The vocabulary of a language (the 'lexicon') is treated not just as a list of words but as a very rich and complex set of associations, a line of thought that will be explored in Chapter 5. Often this approach overlaps with cognitive psychology. The second approach starts with the meaning of sentences, and borrows heavily from ideas in formal logic and philosophy. This approach is often termed formal or TRUTH-CONDITIONAL SEMANTICS, for reasons which will soon become apparent.

    The question is sometimes asked which is the basic unit of meaning in language, the word or the sentence. (There are also intermediate levels which seem to have some significance – phrases like 'the girl in the yellow dress', or to 'cook your goose'.) At one extreme, sentences could be regarded as simply combinations of words. After all, many words ('dog', 'apple', 'hot') have an obvious significance of their own, one which can be grasped for example by children before they learn to deal with sentences. Of course such an approach still has to deal with what the Chinese tradition calls 'empty words' – words like 'the' and 'and' which don't have such an obvious reference but which help to glue the sentence together and contribute to its overall meaning. At the other extreme, sentence meaning can be taken as basic and the semantic content of words (whether full or empty) defined in terms of the contribution they make to that of a sentence.

I have no particular axe to grind on this issue of which comes first. However, this book will start by talking about sentence meaning, and will go on to treat word meaning largely in that context. Another book in this series is devoted to lexical semantics – *Word Meaning* by Richard Hudson.

The important thing to bear in mind is that sentence meaning is different in kind from the meanings of words or phrases. This is not a matter of length – you can have very long words and very short sentences (compare 'antediluvian' and 'Get out!'). The point is that only a sentence can be true or false. A word or phrase by itself cannot (unless it happens to constitute a complete sentence.).

✐ **EXERCISE**

1.10   Say whether or not the following expressions can be true.

    a   'the man who you saw at the bus-stop yesterday'
    b   'I miss you'
    c   'very nice'
    d   'the truth'
    e   'it is not true that I burnt the turkey'
    f   'the fact that they didn't come'

I will assume as a working definition that a sentence is an expression which can be judged true or false (i.e. 'assigned a TRUTH VALUE'). Strictly speaking this applies directly only to certain types of sentence, which I will call 'statements'. (Other kinds of sentences, like questions or commands, require a more indirect approach, which is beyond the scope of this book.) The truth value does not exhaust the meaning of the sentence (we don't want to arrive at a situation where any two true sentences have the same meaning!). But it is the main thing that distinguishes sentence meanings from the meanings of other expressions. It has been said that 'to know the meaning of a sentence is to know what the world would have to be like for the sentence to be true'. This is not uncontroversial, but it will be the starting point for the treatment of sentence meaning which starts in the next chapter.

truth value

**1.5
SUMMARY**

logic

This chapter has taken a preliminary look at the idea of meaning in language, and tried to mark out the area to be covered by 'semantics'. It is concerned mainly with the intrinsic information conveyed by word types and sentence types, in relation to that of other such expressions and to the world which they describe. The closely related field of pragmatics is concerned more with the additional effects associated with the use of an utterance token in a given context.

Sentences are distinguished from other expressions by the fact that they can be judged *true* or *false*, and it was suggested that an important part of the meaning of a sentence involves the ability to assign it one of these truth values on the basis of the facts of the situation it describes. The question of how the truth values of different sentences are related is part of the study of LOGIC – so this is where logic comes into semantics. The next chapter will begin to explore relations between sentences from this point of view.

TRUTH CONDITIONS

2

> 'To know the meaning of a sentence is to know what the world would have to be like for the sentence to be true.'

Suppose we have the following simple sentences, and you want to know whether they are true or false.

    1   'dogs are animals'
    2   'it is raining outside'

In the first case, just looking at the words on the page will be enough to tell you that the statement is true. It is not possible for a dog not to be an animal. In the second case, you cannot tell in advance whether it is true or false. You have to look out of the window. But you know what the world must be like for it to be true, or for it to be false. In other words you know its TRUTH CONDITIONS. Because of this, a glance out of the window is enough to tell you whether the statement is true or not.

    truth conditions

    If the meaning of a sentence is closely related to its truth conditions, then these different ways of determining whether a sentence is true reflect different types of meaning. We will be concerned in due course with both. However for the moment let's focus on the second type.

    Clearly, your answer depends which window you look through, and when. Through the window of my office in London this afternoon, it happens to be true. If I looked through somebody else's window – perhaps that of a friend in Greece – or even through my own window at a different time, it might be false.

    These windows are a convenient way of visualizing the fact that the truth or falsity of a statement like (2) depends on the state of affairs in the world. Some windows will give the verdict *true* and others *false* for any given statement. It may be helpful to think of each window as a 'possible situation' or a 'possible world', in which a particular state of affairs holds.

2.1 1   What is the truth value of the following statements, according to the information in your nearest window? Assume the truth values available are *true* and *false*.
a   'it is snowing.'
b   'there are at least two aeroplanes.'
c   'there is not a cloud in the sky.'

2   Why might the following be difficult to assign a truth value?
a   'it is quite quiet.'
b   'it is a beautiful view.'
c   'there will be a storm tomorrow.'
In general this book will assume that truth values can be assigned as in 1. Obviously cases like those in 2 show the limitations of this assumption. Some of them will be discussed in later chapters.

In more complicated cases we may well be concerned with more than one statement at a time. In (2.2), for example, there are two statements joined by 'and'.

(2.2)   'it is raining and it is cold.'

Let's call the first statement P and the second one Q. Each may be *true* or *false*, which gives us four possibilities. Each row repre- sents one possible combination (a 'window')

(2.3)   P   Q
        t   t
        t   f
        f   t
        f   f

2.4   Describe the state of the world represented by each row.

The whole sentence (2.2) also has its own truth value. Obviously this depends on the truth value assigned to the individual statements *plus the fact that they are connected by 'and'*. The connective 'and' requires that for the overall verdict to be *true*, both individual state- ments have to have the value *true*. Otherwise the overall verdict will be *false*. For each row we can now decide the value for the overall sentence, which we can write as P & Q (2.5).

(2.5) Truth table for 2.2
P = it is raining
Q = it is cold

P	Q	P & Q
t	t	t
t	f	f
f	t	f
f	f	f

Notice that this table effectively provides a truth-conditional definition of the word 'and'. It could be paraphrased as follows:

(2.6) 'And' joins two or more statements to form a composite statement whose truth value is *true* if all the component statements are *true*; otherwise it is *false*.

This is not the only meaning of the English word 'and', but it is an important one, and the one which we will focus on here. It will be written as &, and assumed to have precisely the definition given in (2.6). Symbols like & which can be used to connect statements and give a combined truth value, are termed CONNECTIVES

connectives

The other important connective which can be dealt with in this way is 'or'. Let's take it that in this case the overall verdict is *true* if either or both of the individual statements is true. Sometimes in English we use 'or' to exclude the possibility that both are true, but never mind that for the moment. Imagine a case like (2.7):

(2.7) 'Michael Owen is injured, or he is suspended.'

If either statement happens to be true, then he won't play, and if both happen to be true the overall effect is the same. This is the interpretation of 'or' which will generally be intended in this book. It is generally written ∨, for historical reasons (from Latin 'vel', which covers just this interpretation of 'or' – as opposed to 'aut' which is said to have meant 'either but not both'.)

⬛⬛⬛⬛⬛⬛⬛⬛⬛⬛⬛⬛⬛⬛ *✎* **EXERCISES**

2.8 Draw a truth table like (2.5) for the statements in (2.7). Give an equivalent definition in English, like that in (2.6)

2.9 Draw truth tables for the following sentences (assume that alternatives connected by 'or' are not mutually exclusive):

a 'either the boat capsized or John fell in.'
b 'either Chelsea won and West Ham drew, or Arsenal lost.'
c 'Pooh will have honey and either he will have maple syrup or he will have clotted cream.'

Although these sentences are fairly straightforward, you probably noticed that the order of combining statements can be important. For example (2.10) is ambiguous.

(2.10)   John paid Mary and Mary paid Bill or John paid Bill.

EXERCISE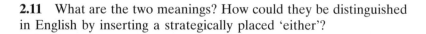

2.11   What are the two meanings? How could they be distinguished in English by inserting a strategically placed 'either'?

The normal way of dealing with this is to put brackets round the expression which is to be evaluated first (just as in arithmetic). Thus (2.10) can be represented as either of the expressions in (2.12).

(2.12)   Two ways of interpreting (2.10):

1   (P & Q) ∨ R
2   P & (Q ∨ R)

Since we said that the sentence had two meanings, we would expect these two expressions to have different truth conditions.

EXERCISE

2.13   Draw the truth tables for both expressions in (2.12) and verify that their truth conditions are different.

What if we want to say the opposite of a particular statement? (Or
negation   better its NEGATION, as we will see later that there are several sorts of opposite.) The simple way of doing this is to reverse the truth values. Thus if P is *true* in a particular window, then its negation ~P is *false*, and vice versa. (Each window must give consistent information.)

(2.14) P	Q	~P	~Q
t	t	f	f
t	f	f	t
f	t	t	f
f	f	t	t

Negation can be combined with the connectives used above. If a composite expression is negated, it is put in brackets. The negation then simply has the effect of reversing all the truth values for that expression.

(2.15)

P	Q	P & Q	~(P & Q)
t	t	t	f
t	f	f	t
f	t	f	t
f	f	f	t

The last column gives the truth conditions for 'it is not the case that both P and Q are true'. Intuitively, this would seem to be the same as saying that either P or Q is false (or both of course).

✎ EXERCISE

2.16 1 Draw a truth table for the latter, to check that it is indeed equivalent.
2 Similarly, 'it is not the case that either P or Q is true' would seem to mean the same as 'both P and Q are false'. Verify this by drawing the truth tables.

Finally, look at the following sentences. Are they true or false?

(2.17) 'she passed the exam and she did not pass the exam.'

(2.18) 'either she passed the exam or she did not pass the exam.'

Taking them at face value, it would seem that we can evaluate these sentences just be looking at them, without knowing anything about the state of the world. We don't even have to know who 'she' or 'the exam' refer to (as long as they are kept constant). Obviously, this is because each sentence is not composed of two *independent* statements, but a single statement and its negation.

The truth table for (2.17) will look like this (2.19).

(2.19)

P	~P	P & ~P
t	f	f
f	t	f

There are only two rows, the second column is determined by the fact that windows must be consistent, and both rows will lead to the overall verdict *false*. Thus a statement of this kind is false regardless of the state of the world.

✎ EXERCISE

2.20 Now draw a similar truth table for (2.18).

Your answer to (2.20) should have two rows, each leading to the overall verdict *true*. Thus a sentence like (2.18) is *true* regardless of the state of the world.

These sentences, (2.17) and (2.18), are the first of many examples where a relationship in the meaning of two expressions determines their truth conditions. In fact many of the most important meaning relations in language can be characterized using truth conditions in this way (Chapter 4).

2.1 SUMMARY

This chapter has begun to explore the idea that the meaning of a sentence is connected with its truth conditions. Some sentences' meanings require that they always be true (or false) regardless of the state of the world. Others depend on the particular state of affairs for their evaluation. When more than one statement has to be evaluated, a number of possible combinations arise, and the overall truth value depends on the combination being considered. The formula for determining the overall truth value depends on the connectives being used to join the statements. So far the connectives &, ∨ and ~ have been introduced. (There are two more to come.) If two expressions have the same meaning, then they have been found to have the same truth conditions. Similarly if an expression has more than one meaning, then each interpretation has different truth conditions.

Because the emphasis so far has been on combinations of statements, each individual statement has been treated as a whole, and no attention has been paid to its internal structure. Basic statements have been treated as 'atoms', with no attempt to cut them up and look inside them. Of course, just as in physics, atoms can be split, and doing so tells us more about why they combine in the way they do. This will be the subject of the next chapter.

2.2 SUPPLE-MENTARY EXERCISES ✎

2.21   Show (by drawing the truth tables) that the following pairs of sentences have the same truth conditions.

a   i   John proposed to Mary, and either she hit him or he banged his head.
   ii   Either John proposed to Mary and she hit him, or else John proposed to Mary and he banged his head.

b   i   Either Colonel Mustard did it, or it was done in the billiards room and it was done with the candlestick.
   ii   Either Colonel Mustard did it or it was done in the billiards room, and (also) either Colonel Mustard did it or it was done with the candlestick.

Satisfy yourself that the pairs do have the same meaning.

2.22   In the examples containing two *independent* statements, there are four possible combinations – the truth table has four rows. Some exercises have involved truth tables with eight rows. How many rows would you need to draw truth tables for the following sentence?

> a   Either John loves Mary and Mary loves Bill, or Mary loves Jack and Jack loves Tina.

Formulate a general rule for the number of rows needed for a sentence containing n independent statements.

2.23   Draw the truth table for the sentence 'John is home and Mary is happy'. Now replace 'and' by 'but'. Draw the truth table again. What are the truth conditions?

2.24   From what has been said so far, it would seem that when two statements are joined by 'and', the order of the statements should be unimportant. Thus the following composite sentences should have the same truth conditions:

> a   Mary went off stage and took her clothes off.
> b   Mary took her clothes off and went off stage.

However, they do not intuitively have the same meaning. What does this suggest about truth conditions and the meaning of 'and'?

2.25   Make a truth table for 'either P or Q but not both' (treat 'but' as &). This is often known as 'exclusive or' (as opposed to ∨ as 'inclusive or').

3 GETTING INSIDE SENTENCES

'The meaning of a whole expression depends on the meaning of its parts, plus the way in which they are put together.'

atomic

In the previous chapter, the basic sentences (represented by P, Q etc. in the truth tables) were treated as ATOMIC, as if they had no internal structure. It was assumed that speakers of English simply 'know' the truth conditions of each basic sentence, as if their minds contained a long list of sentences paired with an equally long list of the corresponding truth conditions. Of course this is not really what happens. This is probably obvious, but it is worth dwelling on two reasons why it cannot be the case.

The first is that any human language is capable of producing an infinite number of sentences, not all of which correspond to anything in our experience. Thus it is easy to produce a bizarre sentence (3.1) which you have almost certainly never heard before. Yet you can process it immediately, and recognize its truth conditions.

(3.1) 'your pet crocodile is still logged in to my computer.'

The second is that it fails to capture basic relationships between different sentences. For example, it would treat the following sentences as unrelated:

(3.2) 1 'John loves Mary.'
2 'Mary loves John.'

Of course at one level this is correct – whether John loves Mary is independent of whether Mary loves John, and so the two statements *should* be assigned their truth conditions independently. Nonetheless we still feel that they are related in meaning. And in other cases, as will be discussed in the next chapter, related sentences may *not* be independent in their truth conditions.

So, what is the internal semantic structure of a sentence? In both sentences in (3.2), we can take it that 'John' and 'Mary' refer to individuals in a straightforward way. This doesn't seem to be a helpful way of treating the verb 'loves', however. Rather than referring to a third individual, it is best thought of as describing a state of affairs that holds between *john* and *mary* (in the first sentence, vice versa in the second). It is not an individual but a RELATION between two indi- **relation** viduals – not only in the intuitive sense but in a technical sense (indeed in a mathematical sense, as will be explained later in the chapter).

✐ **EXERCISE**

3.3 Pick out the expression in each sentence which denotes a relation. How many entities does the relation hold between?

    a   'my sister has eaten my sandwich.'
    b   'the company sent Emil to Albania.'
    c   'Bilbo stole this ring from Gollum.'
    d   'Tokyo is bigger than London.'
    e   'the earth goes round the sun.'

Continuing our atomic metaphor, this relation can be thought of as the nucleus of the meaning of a sentence. It holds the sentence together, both by telling us what kind of state of affairs is being described, and also specifying what individuals are required to play a significant role in the situation. If these requirements are satisfied, and if the relation does indeed hold between the specified individuals, then the statement will be *true*.

The following sentences describe a state of affairs as being true of only one individual. Although this can still be thought of as a one-place relation (a relation with only one individual involved), it is more usual in this case to call it a PROPERTY of that individual **property** (*snoring* is a property of *mary*, etc.).

    (3.4) 1   Mary snores.
            2   Transylvania is beautiful.
            3   John is a doctor.

Each relation (or property) both describes a state of affairs and specifies the roles played in it by individuals. The importance of different roles can be illustrated with two-place relations like *eat*, as in the sentence 'the cat has eaten the goldfish'. An eating situation requires two entities, one to play the ROLE of eating, and the other **role** to play the role of getting eaten. Different languages have different ways of distinguishing which is which; in English, word order is the main way of telling who eats who. Properties also assign roles, though in this case only one; the snoring situation requires a snorer (a role played by Mary in the above example).

There is no generally accepted terminology for classifying roles, though there are several systems on offer. Often terms can be coined using the name of the relation (for example an eating situation might be said to involve an eat-er and an eat-ee). But such devices should not be applied too mechanically.

3.5 Go back over the sentences in (3.3), and describe what roles are required for each relation.

There are a few more things to be aware of about roles at this point. The first is that there are often restrictions on what kind of thing can fill a given role in a situation. For example in an eating situation, the eater must be some sort of life form; and the thing eaten has to be something concrete (an unfortunate word in this context, but I mean that it can't be an abstraction like 'unity' or 'relativity'). See exercise 3.12 for further examples.

A particular case of role assignment is that some roles may need to be assigned to a whole statement. In (3.6), for example, the main relation is *believe*. This holds between a believer (who must be something like a human being) and the thing believed, which will normally be a statement (shown here in square brackets). The latter thus fills a role in the believing situation. However, as a statement in its own right it will also contain its own relation (*snore*) and roles (that of *snorer*, allegedly played by Mary's husband).

   (3.6)   Mary believes [that her husband snores].

Statements analysed in the way I have described are given a special notation, which clearly indicates the way in which they are broken down into relations and entities which fill roles. The name of the relation is written first, and then the role-fillers are listed in brackets (often abbreviated to single lower-case letters). The former is known as the PREDICATE and the latter as its ARGUMENTS:

**predicate
arguments**

   (3.7) •   'John loves Mary.'
         •   love(john, mary) or love(j, m)
         •   (predicate = love; arguments = john, mary)

Notice that the predicate is written as the most basic form of the work ('love', rather than 'loves' or 'loved'). The endings on such words are chiefly grammatical phenomena – they do not affect the relation being described.

3.8 Translate these sentences into predicate-argument notation.

a   'Hawaii is exciting.'
b   'Plato was a genius.'
c   'John admires Bill.'
d   'Bill admires John.'
e   'James is taller than Tina.'
f   'Cerberus barks.'

3.9   Translate these predicate-argument formulas into English.

a   crazy(bill)
b   learn(gertrude, latin)
c   give(john, lindsay, flowers)
d   father_of(richard, henry)
e   square_of(9, 3)
f   play(boris, chess)

In translating between predicate-argument formulas and English (or other languages), you will have noticed that certain clues are given by parts of speech. Relations often correspond to verbs. At other times they correspond to adjectives or other parts of speech introduced by the copula ('to be'). The copula itself is not normally written as part of the relation; it is a grammatical requirement (in English), but does not contribute to the semantic relation. (In many languages such as Chinese or Thai, what English speakers would think of as adjectives can occur on their own without any need for a copula.) The argument places are filled in the examples encountered so far mostly by proper names, though you have already met some exceptions. (It should be stressed that these observations are only rules of thumb, and should not be applied too trustingly.)

Finally, it was mentioned above the relation denoted by a verb like 'love' or 'eat' is a relation in the mathematical sense of the word. A relation in mathematics can be defined in terms of ordered pairs. If the latter term is unfamiliar, it may help to think of a football fixture list, abbreviated to pairs of teams with the convention that the home team comes first. The ordering distinguishes which team has which role – hosts or visitors. Thus part of tonight's fixture list might be represented as follows: (Dynamo Kiev, Sparta Praha), (Steaua Bucuresti, Panathinaikos). (In two weeks' time they will swap roles and the ordering will be reversed.)

The denotation of a (two-place) relation is simply a set of such pairs. Thus the relation *author_of* pairs off Shakespeare with *Hamlet*, Pasternak with *Dr Zhivago* and Kazantzakis with *Zorba the Greek*, among a host of others. The whole set of such pairings is the denotation of *author_of*. Remember that denotation is not all there is to *meaning* (Chapter 1). But part of knowing the meaning of the concept is to be able to pick out instances of it in the world, which will involve pairs of entities standing in the appropriate relation.

EXERCISES ▬▬▬▬▬▬▬▬▬▬▬▬▬▬▬▬▬▬▬▬▬

3.10 Good examples of ordered pairs occur in elliptical sentences in English, such as the following. For each sentence give the relation and the ordered pairs of which it holds.

a   'John wants beer, Bill cider, Mary gin, Sarah lemonade and Sebastian sherry.'
b   'Maria is studying Turkish, Ali Chinese, Suresh Hausa, Noriko Indonesian and Natasha Arabic.'

3.11 On the basis of the sentences below, express the relation *kill* as a set of ordered pairs.

Brutus killed Ceasar; David killed Goliath; Elizabeth I killed Mary Queen of Scots; and Henry VIII killed Thomas Moore, Ann Boleyn and Catherine Howard.

The denotation of a one-place predicate is a property – in this case, this can be seen as not a set of ordered pairs but simply a set of individuals. Thus to say 'Rusty is a dog' is to say that *rusty* is a member of the set of dogs.

3.1 SUMMARY

This chapter has been about the way sentence meanings are composed. The nucleus of its meaning comprises a relation and one or more roles. If the relation holds between the specified role-filling entities then the statement is *true*; if it does not then it is *false*. If the roles are not filled (or not filled appropriately) then the sentence is to a greater or lesser degree anomalous, and hence difficult or impossible to process.

The chapter has also introduced a useful notation which reflects this way of analyzing sentences. The atomic statements of the previous chapter can now be replaced by a predicate with its arguments, thus showing some of the internal structure of sentences. There have already been some instances where this internal structure shows the relationship between certain sentences which intuitively seem to be related in meaning, even though their truth conditions may be independent. This grasp of meaning relations is one of our most important semantic intuitions, and will be explored in the next chapter.

3.2 SUPPLE-
MENTARY
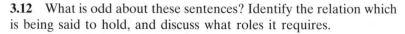

3.12 What is odd about these sentences? Identify the relation which is being said to hold, and discuss what roles it requires.

a   Bill's sister fell a kebab.

    b   My pencil case is talking to you.

    c   I sold my computer to that puddle.

    d   John is giving Mary.

    e   My throat is drinking a glass of wine.

    f   It is raining your umbrella.

3.13 Translate into predicate-argument formulas.

    a   'Jill is a secretary.'

    b   'Shakespeare wrote *Hamlet*.'

    c   'the minister leaked the document to *The Daily Stirrer*.'

    d   'Sheila thinks that Bill is irresponsible.'

    e   'Bruce told Maria that Ruth thinks that Maria stole Nick from Ruth.'

3.14 Translate into English.

    a   bossy(sheila)

    b   capital_of(new_delhi, india)

    c   in(ethiopia, Africa)

    d   near(the_falkland_islands, argentina)

    e   send(john, john's_mother-in-law, australia)

3.15 As predicate-argument formulas correspond to statements, they can be assigned truth values and joined by connectives in the same way as the statements of the previous chapter. Translate these sentences into predicate-argument formulas, and assign them a truth value.

    a   'Spain is warmer than England.'

    b   'Mars is a planet but Jupiter is not a planet.' (Treat 'but' as &).

    c   'Queen Elizabeth is the mother of Prince Charles and Prince Charles is a footballer.'

    d   'It is not the case that either Italy is north of Norway or Gorbachev is an American.'

3.16 Imagine a universe consisting of the following individuals:

Yuri Gagarin   J.F. Kennedy   Gary Kasparov
Marilyn Monroe   Lee Harvey Oswald
Margaret Thatcher

    a   What are the denotations of the following relations or properties?

        russian   woman   kill   lover_of

b   Translate these sentences into predicate-argument notation and give their truth value
i   'Gary Kasparov is Russian.'
ii   'Yuri Gagarin was the lover of Margaret Thatcher.'
iii   'J.F. Kennedy was a woman.'
c   How would you have to change your answers to a in order
to reverse the truth values of b?

MEANING RELATIONS (1)

4

In the previous chapter it was suggested that we have strong intuitions about certain relationships between sentences (and indeed between words).

✎ **EXERCISE**

4.1 Look at the following pairs of sentences, and check that our intuitions agree.

   a   Same meaning (PARAPHRASE)
      i   P – Bill bought this second-hand car from Alex.
      ii   Q – Alex sold this second-hand car to Bill.

   b   Opposite meaning (CONTRADICTION)
      i   P – Maria's husband never does the washing up.
      ii   Q – Maria's husband sometimes does the washing up.

   c   If the first is true, then the second must be (IMPLICATION)
      i   P – Mary has a Burmese cat.
      ii   Q – Mary has a cat

paraphrase

contradiction

implication

If meaning is related to truth conditions, then these relationships in meaning should be expressible in terms of what the world must be like for the sentences to be true. This means that these pairs of sentences cannot be assigned their truth-conditions independently. Thus if a is a genuine paraphrase, no window will ever tell us that one is true and the other false. For b, by contrast, no window will tell us that both are true.

   The third pair c is a particularly important type: it is not possible for P to be *true* and Q *false*. (Of course it is possible for Q to be true and P to be false – that is another matter. We can have a world in which Mary's cat is Siamese.) This third type of relation (implication) plays a basic role in characterizing meaning relations. To capture this, we will add another connective for our truth tables: implication, written '→'. The first two rows capture what we have just said, namely that the relation P → Q only holds if it is not possible for P to be true and Q false.

(4.2) | P | Q | P→Q |
|---|---|---|
| t | t | t |
| t | f | f |
| f | t | t |
| f | f | t |

It is important to remember here that we are not trying to fully capture the meaning of the English word 'implies', but are setting up a new technical term to do a particular job. We need a term which means precisely that it is not possible for P to be true and Q false. This is what is done in (4.2) – no more and no less.

Suppose P is 'it is cold' and Q is 'the cat curls up in front of the fire'. If it is cold, then we expect to find the cat in front of the fire (the state of affairs in row 1). If the cat is not in front of the fire (row 2) then that goes directly against the claim P → Q, so that particular row is excluded (it is a 'counter-example'). If it is not cold (rows 3 and 4) then it does not matter much what the cat is doing – neither state of affairs offers a counter-example to P → Q.

As with the connectives in Chapter 2, it is helpful to also give a definition in words (4.3).

(4.3)   '→' joins two statements P and Q to form a composite statement P → Q whose value is *true* unless P is *true* and Q *false*.

EXERCISE ✎

4.4   a   I claimed that the truth table for P → Q is exactly the same as 'it is not the case that P is true and Q is false'. Draw the truth table for the latter expression, and verify that it does indeed work out the same.

b   Another useful way of putting the same thing is 'either P is false or Q is true'. Check that this too is equivalent.

So now we have our new tool. We can now use it to give a definition of the paraphrase and contradiction relations. First paraphrase, where two sentences are judged to have the same meaning.

Two sentences P and Q are paraphrases if P implies Q and Q implies P. This relation can be written P ↔ Q (suggesting 'mutual implication') or P ≡ Q ('equivalence'); the two mean the same thing. This gives us another connective (the last one!).

The contradiction relation is slightly more complicated. It suggests 'opposite meaning', but 'opposite' in normal usage has at least two different senses. For example, what is the opposite of sentence a in (4.5)? Both b and c can be thought of as 'opposites', but in different ways.

(4.5)   Different kind of opposites:

1   Maria's husband never does the washing up.
2   Maria's husband always does the washing up.
3   Maria's husband sometimes does the washing up.

Of these sentences a and b obviously can not both be true, but it is possible (perhaps even likely) that neither is true. In this case it is because the two lie at two extremes, but we will see examples where the same situation arises for different reasons. Comparing a and c however, it would seem that while both cannot be true, one of them must be; the two complement each other in the same way as P and ~P complement each other (on the assumption we have been using so far – that for any statement P, either P or ~P must be true). I will call the first of these relationships INCOMPATIBILITY   **incompatibility** and the second one contradiction (in traditional logic incompatible statements of the kind exemplified here are called 'contraries').

Two sentences P and Q are incompatible if P implies ~Q and Q implies ~P. P and Q are contradictory if P is equivalent to ~Q (and Q is equivalent to ~P).

You should check that you have absorbed the material in the last few paragraphs before reading on. The following exercise will help you.

✐ **EXERCISE**

4.6   1   Verify that 'P implies Q and Q implies P' ensures that either they are both true or they are both false. (In other words, the definition given for paraphrases gives the right truth conditions.)
2   Verify that 'P implies ~Q and Q implies ~P' gives the right truth conditions for incompatible statements (they cannot both be true but they may both be false).
3   Verify that 'P is equivalent to ~Q' gives the right truth conditions for contradictory statements (one must be true and the other false). You can use the connective ≡; take its truth values from the answer to 1.

In characterizing meaning relations in this way, we have again been treating sentences as atomic. However, in many cases these relations between sentences are the result of relations holding at a lexical level between their component parts.

(4.7)   Implication

1   P – 'Tiny is an alsatian.'
2   Q – 'Tiny is a dog.'

Clearly in (4.7) P implies Q, and equally clearly this is because of a meaning relation between the two predicates, namely that *alsatian* is a kind of *dog*. The relation between these two word senses cannot be called implication, because we have defined implication as a relation between truth values, and predicates by themselves are not the kind of thing that have truth values (only statements do). The corresponding relation between word senses is called HYPONYMY. (The terminology for lexical relations generally involves -onym, from a Greek root meaning *name*.) In the examples (4.7), *alsatian* is a hyponym of *dog*. The following is a natural definition of hyponym:

hyponomy

A is a hyponym of B if it is impossible for an entity to be A without also being B.

For example, *alsatian* is a hyponym of *dog* because it is impossible for something to be an alsatian without also being a dog.

Notice that this definition effectively makes use of the idea of an implication holding between statements; this is typical in showing the close correspondence between lexical relations and sentential ones.

sets

Another useful way of looking at hyponymy makes use of SETS. It was suggested in the previous chapter that the denotation of a predicate should be thought of as a set. Thus while 'Tiny' denotes an individual, 'alsatian' denotes the set of all alsatians, and 'dog' the set of all dogs. Of the sentences in (4.7), 1 is true if the individual *tiny* is a member of the set of alsatians, while 2 is true if he is a member of the set of dogs. To say that *alsatian* is a hyponym of *dog*

subset

is to say that the set of alsatians is a SUBSET of the set of dogs, so that it is impossible to be a member of the first without also being a member of the second. This can be illustrated by a Venn diagram (4.8), in which A represents the set of alsatians, B the set of dogs, and the cross any random individual.

(4.8)

In both sentences of (4.7) the predicate was a one-place relation (or property), so that its denotation was an ordinary set of individuals. For a two-place relation exactly the same holds, except that the set denoted is a set of ordered pairs, as outlined at the end of the previous chapter. For a three-place relation it will be a set of ordered triples, and so on. (It is rare to find predicates with more than three arguments in natural language.)

✎ **EXERCISE**

4.9 For the following pairs of statements, state which predicate is a hyponym of which. Express the hyponymity relationship in each case as a relationship between sets.

    a   i   'Mary's face was red.'
        ii 'Mary's face was crimson.'

    b   i   'Mary slapped John.'
        ii 'Mary hit John.'

    c   i   'John walked home.'
        ii 'John lurched home.'

    d   i   'the secretary shredded the documents.'
        ii 'the secretary cut up the documents.'

    e   i   'the godfather gave Roberto his instructions.'
        ii 'the godfather handed Roberto his instructions.'

Synonyms were defined in Chapter 1 as word forms which have at least one sense in common. We would expect that (when used in this sense) they will denote the same set.

    (4.10) 1   'Mary is truthful.'
            2   'Mary is honest.'

It is impossible to be truthful without being honest, *and vice versa.* Thus *truthful* is a hyponym of *honest* and vice versa. The two word senses denote the same set. (In set theory, two sets are equal if and only if each is a subset of the other.) Moreover it is obvious that this lexical relation is responsible for the fact that the two sentences in (4.10) are paraphrases.

If two words have opposite meanings they are called ANTONYMS. However it was noted above in relation to sentences that 'opposite' has at least two different senses. The same is true of word meaning.

antonyms

    (4.11) 1   John is happy.
            2   John is unhappy.

    (4.12) 1   Mary is a smoker.
            2   Mary is a non-smoker.

In the first case (4.11) it is not possible that John is both happy and unhappy, but it is possible that he is neither. In the other case (4.12), one of the predicates must hold of any individual (assume for the time being that only human individuals are under consideration).

In (4.11), the sets denoted by *happy* and *unhappy* are completely separate (disjoint). There are no individuals in the intersection between them. However, there may be individuals which are outside both sets (4.13) (This is not the whole of the story for these antonyms – see the supplementary exercises.)

(4.13)

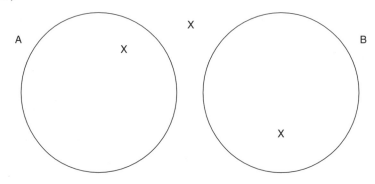

In (4.12) each set is the complement of the other: they are disjoint (as before), but this time together they take up the entire space under consideration, and each individual must be in one or the other (4.14).

(4.14)

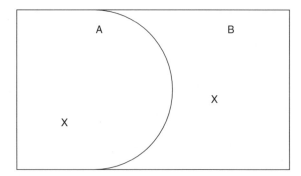

For want of better terminology I will refer to the two types as incompatible antonyms and contradictory antonyms.[1] The presence of the word antonym is to serve as a reminder that we are talking about a lexical relationship and not a sentential one.

Notice how these lexical relations parallel the sentential ones defined earlier in the chapter (with the subset relation ⊆ corresponding to →).

(4.15)

Hyponymy	A ⊆ B	Implication	P → Q
Synonymy	A ⊆ B and B ⊆ A	Paraphrase	(P → Q) & (Q → P)
Antonymy i	A ⊆ ~B and B ⊆ ~A	Incompatibility	(P → ~Q) & (Q → ~P)
Antonymy ii	A = ~B	Contradiction	P ≡ ~Q

✎ EXERCISE

4.16 Are the following pairs of antonyms incompatible or contra-dictory? Explain why, using sets.

a   vegetarian meat-eater
b   blue red
c   European Asian
d   married unmarried

This chapter has examined basic meaning relations. At the senten-tial level the relation of implication can be used to characterize a variety of relations including paraphrase, incompatibility and contra-diction. This analysis is based on truth values, as in Chapter 2.

Looking inside sentences, it was found that similar relations hold between word senses (specifically those of predicates). The relation of hyponomy corresponds to implication (but holds between word senses, not statements or truth values).

If the denotations of predicates are regarded as sets, then hyponyms can be interpreted as subsets. This approach, as illustrated by Venn diagrams, is often a useful model to have in mind when considering word meaning. The next chapter will examine word meanings in more detail.

4.1 SUMMARY

4.2   SUPPLE-MENTARY EXERCISES

valid

4.17 The following are popular forms of argument, some sound and some not. Use truth tables to show which ones are VALID (guaran-teed to be true).

a   If P implies Q, and P is true, then Q is true.
b   If P implies Q, and P is not true, then Q is not true.
c   If P implies Q, and Q is not true, then P is not true.
d   If P or Q is true, and P is not true, then Q is true.

Make up examples of your own for each of these patterns

4.18 The following pairs are all incompatible as defined; but not all of them would naturally be considered pairs of antonyms. Which pairs would? Suggest other criteria we need besides incompatibility.

a i John is a *doctor*
  ii John is an *aardvark*

b i Mary is *shouting*
  ii Mary is *whispering*

c i You should paint the whole thing *red*
  ii You should paint the whole thing *turquoise*

d i Dark Rum is a *stallion*
  ii Dark Rum is a *mare*

4.19 In (4.7), the implication relation went in the same direction as the hyponymity relation. In the following examples it goes in the opposite direction. Draw the Venn diagrams and explain why.

a i Tiny is not a dog.
  ii Tiny is not an alsatian.

b i They want to ban drink.
  ii They want to ban beer.

c i Sport is forbidden.
  ii Football is forbidden.

NOTE

1 Many books refer to them simply as 'antonyms' and 'contradictories' respectively.

MEANING RELATIONS (2)

5

It was suggested in Chapter 1 that the sense of an expression can be seen as a way of classifying things. (I deliberately leave the word 'things' as vague as possible, because to call them anything else would suggest that they have already been classified!). Thus the word 'book', used of the thing you now have in front of you, refers to it as a *book*, i.e. an instantiation of a particular bundle of properties which are shared by other books, but not by cats, or chocolates.

This classification however does not consist of just putting objects into arbitrary pigeon-holes. The hyponym relation means that an object can be classified at a more general level or at a more specific level. For example *textbook* is a hyponym of *book* (or let's say *book*₁, as there may be other senses associated with the English word 'book'). *Book*₁ can be used to classify more objects than *textbook* can. But *textbook* is more informative; it pins the object down more precisely. This flexibility allows you to classify an object in different ways depending on how much information it is desirable to commit yourself to in the context.

The hyponym relation between senses should be distinguished carefully from the relation between a sense and the individuals which it classifies (its denotation). The object in front of you 'is a' textbook, and also 'is a' book, in that it instantiates (is an INSTANCE of) these word senses. On the other hand a textbook (or more precisely the concept *textbook*) is a kind of *book*, in that it is a species or type of book. In artificial intelligence the two different relations are sometimes known by the mnemonics 'isa' and 'ako' respectively. These simple relations can be used to build up a 'semantic network'.

instance

(5.1)

5.2   Draw semantic networks based on the following concepts (word senses) and named objects:

a   mammal mouse babe micky pig animal
b   london new_york country city france capital tokyo place port
c   jane_eyre film star_wars novel book story crime_and_punishment

What exactly the 'bundle of properties' is which defines each of these concepts is a complicated question. For example, why do you call this object in front of you a 'book'? Probably because it is made of sheets of paper in a particular configuration, and is covered with markings which are the written form of a known human language. Because of this, you can infer that a reasonable thing to do with it is to read it, and not to eat it or stroke it. But suppose you saw the same writing in electronic form on my computer screen? Or conversely if you opened the book and it contained no writing. Would you still call it a book? Probably. The two have no obvious properties in common, but both have a resemblance (a different resemblance) to the book you are reading. This notion of 'resemblance' appears to play an important part in how things are classified.

There is another related question: how much of the information that goes into the lexicon (or into a semantic network) is information about words (senses) and how much is about facts. This was touched on in Chapter 1, where it was suggested that knowing the meaning of a word shouldn't depend too much on knowledge of 'trivia' (i.e. facts!). This is often put by linguists in terms of a distinction between 'lexical' and 'encyclopaedic' knowledge. This exploits the difference between a lexicon (or mental dictionary) and an encyclopaedia, which is pretty well entrenched in our culture. But is there a difference in principle, or is it only a matter of degree? For example, knowing the meaning of the word 'elephant' would involve some idea of an elephant's characteristic shape and size, whereas the fact that it evolved in Asia and Africa might reasonably be assigned to an encyclopaedia. But other details of an animal's anatomy, evolutionary history and habitat might seem to fall somewhere between the two. (Compare polar bears, for example, where the name itself makes reference to the habitat.)

✐ **EXERCISE**

5.3 List three facts you can infer from each of these sentences. Would you expect to find them in a dictionary or an encyclopedia entry under the word in italics? Or neither?

    a   Mary is a *mathematician.*
    b   This is a photograph of a *nebula.*
    c   Lobsters are related to *sea-scorpions.*
    d   John is becoming a *Buddhist.*

Certainly one important point about classifying things with words is that it enables you to draw certain conclusions about the objects. If you know that an object is classified by the word *snake*, then a natural reaction is to give it a wide berth. The word seems to associate the information about a thin wriggly object with a scenario which involves getting bitten. Moreover because of language we are able to acquire this anti-snake prejudice without ever having seen one.

It is worth dwelling a little on this because, despite the so-called logical basis of language, the logic behind it is not at all obvious. It is not true that all snakes will bite humans, only that some snakes will. (It is also true that some snakes are green, but this does not lead to an assumption that all snakes are green.) What seems to be at work here is that some pieces of information about snakes are picked out as being particularly important, and made into part of a stereotype. Obviously this ability to form stereotypes has a certain survival value, even though the chain of reasoning involved is dubious. An organism whose brain was programmed with first order logic wouldn't follow this reasoning. (On the other hand such an organism might not last long.)

Thus, classifying an object by a given word sense is felt to have certain consequences, but these consequences are not so hard-and-fast as the implications we were looking at in earlier chapters. Take the sentence 'if it is a snake then it bites'. On the basis of what was said about implications, we would not expect to find any case of a snake that does not bite. Since there are such cases, the implication does not hold. Nonetheless there is an 'expectation' that a snake will bite, and a snake which does not is felt to be less typical than a snake which does. A good way of testing for expectations involves the conjunctions 'so' and 'but':

  (5.4) 1 'That is a snake, so it will bite.'
      2 'That is a snake, but it won't bite.'

If you change the conjunctions round, it sounds strange:

  (5.5) 1 ? 'That is a snake, but it will bite.'
      2 ? 'That is a snake, so it won't bite.'

And if it is used for information which is not related to the stereotype, the result is odd whichever conjunction is used.

  (5.6) 1 ? 'That is a snake, but it is green.'
      2 ? 'That is a snake, so it is green.'

EXERCISE ✎

5.7 What expectations would you associate with the following concepts? Test them using the conjunctions 'so' and 'but'.

city	priest	comedy	nazi	library
alsatian	professor	dolphin	bestseller	teenager
feminist				

So where does all this leave the idea that the denotation of a word sense can be modelled as a set (Chapter 4)? At the very least we now have to distinguish between the typical members which form **prototype** the core of the set (many writers use the term PROTOTYPE) and others which are untypical in some way. Often the untypicality of these entities can be traced to their membership of a particular subset, which is the denotation of a hyponym. This subset may have its own built-in expectations. Thus *penguin* is a hyponym of *bird*; but whereas birds are expected to be able to fly, penguins are not:

  (5.8) 1 'That is a penguin, so it can't fly.'
      2 'That is a penguin, but it can fly.' (A magic penguin)

What this tells us is that the expectations associated with a more specific word sense cancel out (or take priority over) those of a more general concept. In this case the relevant hyponym or subset was ready-made for us, but in most cases it is possible to make one anyway by combining words. For example we can make a set of *flightless_birds,* which will be a subset of *birds* to which the expectation of flightlessness applies. At the same time the use of such phrases seems to emphasize the expectation of flight associated with birds in general. A good example of this effect is the phrase 'working mother', which has been objected to as perpetuating certain stereotypes about mothers.

The 'expectations' associated with word senses are often known **default** as DEFAULT inferences, and can be studied using a suitably adapted logic called default logic. Such logics are unfortunately beyond the scope of this book, but they are playing an increasingly important part in semantics research. The idea is that such an inference holds 'provided there is no information that is incompatible with the conclusion'. Thus if Tweety is a bird, then we can infer that Tweety flies – provided we do not know that Tweety is a flightless bird, say a penguin.

5.9 Look again at your answers to (5.7) and find subclasses to which the expectations you listed might not apply.

In a semantic network, all the properties associated with a concept are automatically associated also with any concept which stands in an 'ako' relation with it (i.e. all its hyponyms). For example, the concept *animal* involves being able to move, needing to eat, and so on. A pig has these same properties precisely because it is an animal. We can say that it INHERITS these properties from the more general concept of which it is a hyponym. (It also introduces extra properties of its own, like having a curly tail.)

inherits

  A concept can be a hyponym of several more general concepts at once. For example, *coin* is a kind of metallic object and at the same time a kind of medium of exchange. It will inherit from both of these more general concepts. So on the one hand it has a particular economic value, and on the other hand it has the properties associated with a metallic object.

5.10 List two or three properties associated with the following concepts, and try to find more general concepts from which these properties are inherited. (These more general concepts need not correspond to a single word.)

tree   gold   murder   red   mackerel   miner
bulldozer   triangle

The focus of this chapter has been on lexical meaning relations, and to what extent these follow the logical patterns outlined at the end of the last chapter. Word meanings are related by networks sometimes known as SEMANTIC NETWORKS. These relations are responsible for expectations which enable us to draw certain conclusions. However, in many cases these conclusions cannot be drawn firmly but only by default.

**5.1
SUMMARY**

semantic networks

5.11 One kind of antonymy occurs when one predicate expresses the same relation as the other but with the arguments reversed – the CONVERSE of the relation (Chapter 3). Give converses for the following predicates, and state both sentences as predicate-argument formulas.

    a   12 is twice 6.
    b   Tokyo is bigger than London.
    c   Chomsky was a student of Harris.
    d   Elizabeth I succeeded Mary.
    e   Belgrade is below Vienna (on the Danube).

5.12 Strictly speaking only two-place relations have converses. However some three-place predicates are related by a similar permutation of their arguments (e.g. 'John gave the book to Mary' vs 'Mary received the book from John'). Imagine the following scenario: Don Marino hands Antonio a gun, and Antonio hands Don Marino a thousand dollars. Express this using the three-place verbs 'buy', 'sell', 'cost' and 'fetch'.

5.13 The levels of a semantic network do not seem to have the same status. Study the following examples.

    a   The following form part of a semantic network:

        labrador   dog   bitch   mammal
        animal   quadruped

      i   Draw the network
      ii   It was suggested above that properties were 'inherited' by more specific nodes from more general nodes. What are the most general nodes introducing the following properties, and which hyponyms inherit them?
        1   Need for exercise.
        2   Ability to suckle offspring.
        3   Having four legs.
      iii   Which words fit more naturally into the following sentences:
        1   It's time to take my [ ] for a walk.
        2   Look at that [ ] suckling its puppies.
        3   My [ ] is on heat.
        4   That [ ] is limping around on three legs.
    Which word would you *expect* the properties described to be associated with, given your answers to a(ii)?

THINGS AND EVENTS

6

At the top level (the most general level) of a semantic network, most word senses can be grouped under certain extremely general concepts such as *thing* or *event*. These have certain important semantic characteristics, which have important effects on the ways in which they can be expressed in language. It will be convenient to discuss them by taking nouns and verbs in turn – though you should be careful of assuming that this distinction always corresponds to that between things and events.

First consider the following scenario, and the various ways in which it might appropriately be described. A dragon has his eye on a hoard of treasure, comprising gold rings.

(6.1) 1 (a) *The dragon saw a gold.
          (b) The dragon saw some gold.
          (c) *The dragon saw some golds.
          (d) The dragon saw a heap/some heaps of gold.

       2 (a) The dragon saw a ring.
          (b) *The dragon saw some ring.
          (c) The dragon saw some rings.
          (d) The dragon saw a heap/some heaps of rings.

This shows that 'gold' and 'ring' are acceptable in different kinds of syntactic environment. This is due, however, to an important *semantic* difference. The point is that gold is conceptualized as a substance, whereas artefacts like rings are thought of as individual items. This correlates with a number of differences, both linguistic and non-linguistic. For example rings are countable in a straightforward way, whereas you can only compare quantities of gold by introducing some notion of measure (even a crude measure like a *heap* that a dragon might be able to individuate). Moreover if you divide gold into pieces each piece remains *gold*, whereas if you break up a ring what you have left is not a ring. However if you scatter *rings* (in the plural) over the floor of your cave they still remain rings – plurals of countable nouns behave in some respects like uncountable ones, both logically and grammatically (6.1).

A good test is provided by the phrase 'all over (something)'.[1] It will accept mass nouns like gold but not countable nouns (unless they are plural, in which case they can be distributed without losing their identity).

(6.2) 1   There was gold all over the floor.
       2   ?? There was ring all over the floor.
       3   There were rings all over the floor.

Note that the second sentence is not completely unacceptable, but it forces an unusual reading, in which 'ring' is re-interpreted as a mass (perhaps the dragon has breathed on it and melted it). This effect generally occurs with countable nouns in this environment.

(6.3) 1   The pro-director ended up with *sandwich* all over his face.
       2   After the accident there was *dog* all over the road.

EXERCISE ✎

6.4 Which of these nouns are countable and which are 'mass' nouns? For the latter, suggest a suitable 'measure word'.

| coal | sheep | news | money | lamb | sugar |
| iron | rice | beer | chocolate | information |

construal

6.5 When a mass noun is treated as a countable noun, again a re-interpretation is forced (this is often referred to as CONSTRUAL). How are the mass nouns 'whisky' and 'wine' construed in these sentences?

1   This really is a fine whisky.
2   We've got some new wines in this year.

(The examples in (6.1) and (6.4) are syntactic facts about English, but the underlying semantic difference between countable and mass nouns is an important one which is reflected in different ways in many languages.)

The situations described by verbs also have important distinctions (important to us, once again, because they are reflected in language). The first is between states and events.

(6.6) 1   Istanbul overlooks the Bosporus.
       2   The child was asleep.
       3   Mozart died in 1791.
       4   One of the soldiers coughed.

In the first two sentences nothing is happening. The sentences describe states – the first one permanent, the second temporary. In the latter case presumably the child has fallen asleep and will wake up again, but the sentence ignores these events. It is like a still photograph (as opposed to a movie). The last two sentences, by contrast, describe events. Predicates describing events are normally verbs. Those describing states may be verbs, or they may be other expressions attached with a copula (recall that this happens to be a grammatical requirement in English).

It is important to distinguish between states which are a permanent property of an individual (or relation between individuals) and those which merely describe a phase they are going through. A good example is this well-known exchange involving Winston Churchill:

> (6.7)   'Mr Churchill, you are drunk.'
>   'You, Madam, are ugly. And tomorrow – I shall be sober.'

At least as used here, *ugly* is assumed to be an intrinsic property of an individual, which is arguably how language tends to treat it (whether or not this is literally true). One test is that intrinsic properties co-occur naturally with generalized statements about classes of individuals:

> (6.8)   1   'Snakes are poisonous.'
>   2 ?? 'Snakes are asleep.'
>   3   'Semanticists are ugly.'
>   4 ?? 'Semanticists are drunk.'

The last two statements are about equally reasonable (or unreasonable) things to want to say, but linguistically 3 holds together much better than 4. This is because of the difference between intrinsic properties and temporary phases.[2]

If STATIVE predicates (predicates describing states) are like a still photograph, it shouldn't be surprising that EVENTIVE predicates may represent a change from one state to another, like two successive slides.

**stative
eventive**

✐ **EXERCISE**

6.9 How would you characterize the states before and after each of these events?

    a   The plane took off.
    b   Louise tidied her room.
    c   Gandalf lit a fire.
    d   Toad arrived at the party.
    e   The hobbit disappeared.

How much do the sentences tell us about the way the change is effected?

At the other end of the scale we have verbs which describe an action or activity, but may not tell us much about the result (if any). Typically the hyponyms of these verbs will give us more detail about the manner in which the action is carried out. (In this case it might be better to gloss the hyponym relation as 'a way of' rather than 'a kind of'.)

EXERCISE

6.10   Suggest some hyponyms for the verbs in italics. What extra information would they give?

a   The men *walked* down the corridor.
b   The tyrant liked to *kill* his enemies.
c   Paul *asked* Louise to lend him some money.
d   When she had finished she *told* the answer to Mary.
e   The vandals spent half an hour *hitting* the sculptures.

How much do the hyponyms tell us about the result of the action?

In most of these cases you could take a snapshot of the action in progress, as if frozen in time. Clearly it would be a much more vivid snapshot if one of the hyponyms were chosen. The hyponyms tell us more about the characteristic manner of an action, or some instrument that is used, and a picture or charade showing this is often all we need in order to understand what action is taking place.

In many cases (like the first sentence in (6.10)), the situation described by the verb can be characterized purely in these terms. These may be called 'ACTIVITY verbs'. These have a number of syntactic and semantic properties.

activity

Take an instance of an activity like that denoted by 'walk' in 'John and Mary walked on the beach'. Any part of the time covered by that activity can also be described by the sentence 'John and Mary walked on the beach'. This is rather like the situation with *gold* described above, where if you have any quantity of *gold*, any part of it is also *gold*.

EXERCISE

6.11   Which of the following sentences have this property?

a   The plane circled over the airfield.
b   Katia danced beautifully.
c   Maria cleared the table.
d   The men hammered at the sheet of metal.
e   The ship sailed round the world.

Another striking feature of activities appears if the verb form in these sentences is replaced by the verb form 'was ... -ing'. This has the effect of freezing the action at a particular point of time, as in the snapshots described earlier.

(6.12) 1 John and Mary walked on the beach.
     2 John and Mary were walking on the beach.

These two sentences imply each other, and thus have the same truth conditions. If they walked on the beach, then at any given time they were walking on the beach, and could be photographed doing so. Conversely if we know that at some point they were walking on the beach, then we can assert that they walked on the beach.

✎ **EXERCISE**

6.13 Apply this test to the sentences in (6.11). Does it yield the same results as the previous test?

If the action includes the idea of a change of state, then this no longer holds, precisely because the change of state implies that the action is completed. Seeing earlier stages of the action in progress does not imply that the action was ever completed. (Arriving at a destination is a particular case of a change of state, which might be termed 'change of location'.)

(6.14) 1 John ran to the phone box.
     2 John was running to the phone box.

Here the implication only holds in one direction – the second sentence does not imply that John ever made it. He could have tripped over and ended up in hospital instead. Equally if you take one stage of his running to the phone box, that cannot be described by the sentence 'he ran to the phone box'. Only the complete action can. This is analogous to the situation with countable nouns: only a complete ring is a ring, a fragment of it is only a bit of gold.

Events which specify a point where the action is complete – for example a change of state or location – are known as TELIC (the opposite is ATELIC). **telic** **atelic**

Given these parallels between things and events, it is not surprising that sometimes the two interact.

✎ **EXERCISE**

6.15 Applying the tests you have studied in this chapter, state whether the expressions in square brackets are count or mass nouns. Then test whether the events described are telic or atelic. What is the correlation between the two results?

a   The orchestra played [music].
b   The orchestra played [a symphony].
c   The orchestra played [symphonies]
d   The orchestra played [three symphonies].

6.1 SUMMARY

This chapter has looked at ways in which language structures things and events, two of the cornerstones of the way it analyses the world. Some simple examples have been given of the way in which the grammatical structure of a language (English) is sensitive to these underlying semantic considerations.

Often, it is the semantic requirements of an event that dictate what elements you can actually have in a sentence. This was discussed from a different point of view in Chapter 3, where the roles required by a situation determine how many arguments a predicate should have. It will also be the main theme of the final chapter (9).

Several times in the last few chapters you have encountered arguments which are not individual names but phrases like 'all snakes' or 'three symphonies'. The next chapter will discuss ways of dealing with such expressions.

6.2 SUPPLE-MENTARY EXERCISES ✎

6.16   Are the following actions telic or atelic?

lock   tie   appear   cover   embark   connect

Many verbs have the opposite meaning when 'un-' or 'dis-' is added. (This particular kind of antonym is known as a 'reversive'.) What is reversed in each case, an activity or a change of state?

6.17   Look at the following sentences

a   i   Maria hit him, then she hit him again.
    ii   The light flashed, then it flashed again.

b   iii The ice melted, then it froze again.
    iv   The water froze, then it melted again.

What does 'again' contribute in each case? Why is the effect different in the second pair of sentences?

6.18   Look at how the following sentences can be built up. At each stage are they telic or atelic? Try to isolate what it is that has this effect in each case.

a   i   John and Harry lurched along.
    ii   John and Harry lurched along to the club.
    iii John and Harry lurched along to the club every night.

    iv   John and Harry lurched along to the club every night
        for two months.

b   i   The light flashed.
    ii   The light flashed for two hours.
    iii   The light flashed for two hours every night.
    iv   The light flashed for two hours every night for a week

c   i   Laura cried.
    ii   Laura cried herself to sleep.
    iii   Laura cried herself to sleep every night.
    iv   Laura cried herself to sleep every night for a week.

6.19   It was noted above (Exercise 2.24) that two statements joined by '&' sometimes have different truth conditions if you reverse the order. To which of these examples does this apply? Suggest an explanation.

    a   Louise sang and danced.
    b   Louise was singing and dancing.
    c   Eleni drank a bottle of retsina and fell asleep.
    d   Eleni was drinking a bottle of retsina and falling asleep.
    e   Budapest is below Vienna and above Belgrade.

NOTES

1   Except when dealing with certain abstract nouns, to which concepts of location and distribution may not apply.
2   If you introduce the word 'always' judgements may change. This is because you are introducing an element of *time*, which goes better with temporary states.

7 QUANTIFIERS (1)

In the following extract, Odysseus has told Polyphemus the Cyclops that his name is 'Nobody'. Polyphemus believes him, which leads to frustrating results when he has to call for help from his neighbours. What is the essence of the misunderstanding?

> 'What's up, Polyphemus? Who's hurting you?'
>
> 'Nobody's hurting me. Nobody has just gouged my eye out.'
>
> 'Well if nobody's hurting you, shut up and let us get some sleep.'

Obviously, the other Cyclopes do not understand 'nobody' as referring to an individual as Polyphemus intends. So what does it refer to? What is *nobody*, and how, for example, does it differ from *nothing*?

Up to now we have been treating a predicate as denoting a relation between individuals. However, in the following sentences (7.1), this strategy does not seem to be possible. Obviously, the denotations of 'everybody' and 'nobody' cannot be treated as individuals on a par with the denotations of 'John', 'Mary' or 'the president'.

(7.1) 1 Nobody loves Mary
       2 Somebody loves Mary
       3 Everybody loves Mary

quantifiers

Words like 'all', 'some' and 'none' are called QUANTIFIERS (perhaps unhelpfully, as not all them involve any obvious notion of quantity). They are not the only ones (in fact there are a literally infinite number), but they occupy a special place for many reasons. This is reflected by the fact that in many languages, as in the English examples above, there are special words expressing their combinations with people and things (cf. 'everything', 'something', 'nothing'; whereas we don't have 'threething', 'manything' or 'tenbody').

44

In Chapter 4, hyponym relations were defined in terms of subsets. If *cricketer* is a hyponym of *sportsperson* then the set of cricketers is a subset of the set of sportspeople. Conversely the antonym relation was represented by disjoint sets. If *militarist* and *pacifist* are antonyms, then there is no overlap (intersection) between the two sets.

Something similar to this is going on with quantifiers. The lexical relations just mentioned could be expressed as 'all cricketers are sportspeople', and 'no militarists are pacifists'. But precisely because these are lexical relations, they don't make very informative statements about the world; they are true 'by definition'. A more interesting claim might be 'all Australians are sportspeople', or 'no Conservatives are pacifists'. These are not statements about the meaning of words but claims about the situation in the world. However they are like the lexical relations in claiming a particular relation between two sets, the subset relation in the first case and disjointness in the second – but this time as empirical facts, not as something pre-packaged in the lexicon. (Another difference is that the use of 'all' or 'none' does not allow exceptions, whereas as we have seen, lexical meaning relations often do.)

The first step we can take, therefore, is to treat quantifiers as denoting a relation between two sets. 'All' denotes the subset relation between two sets – in the example given, the set of Australians and the set of sportsmen.

(7.2)

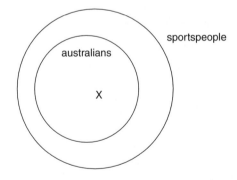

The quantifiers 'some' and 'no(-ne)' can be treated in a similar way. Suppose at the other extreme we wonder whether *any* Australians are sportspeople. We have a set of Australians and a set of sportspeople; the question is whether there are any individuals who answer to both descriptions. This is the same as asking whether the two sets have an intersection. The statement 'some Australians are sportspeople' claims that there is one. The statement 'no Australians are sportspeople' claims that there isn't.[1]

(7.3)

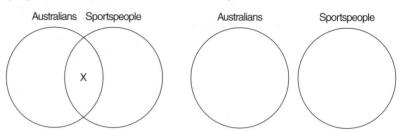

Along with quantifiers, this approach gives us a way of dealing with 'common nouns' (words like 'dog', 'book', 'Australian' or 'Conservative'). Up to now we have only been able to deal with them when they have occurred as predicates ('John is an Australian', etc.). Now we have a way of approaching them when they occur, with a quantifier, as part of the *argument*. And they still have the same denotation that they had as a predicate (namely a set) – which at least shows we're being consistent.

EXERCISE ✎

7.4 Draw Venn diagrams illustrating the relations between sets which are claimed by the following sentences:

    a   'all students smoke' (or 'all students are smokers').
    b   'some snakes are poisonous.'
    c   'no cities are pleasant.'

The same idea can be extended to include most of the other quantifiers found in natural language. For example, the numerals.

    (7.5) 1   Five planets are visible to the naked eye.
          2   126 Conservatives are Euro-sceptics.

The first indicates that there are five objects which are both planets and are visible to the naked eye. In other words the set of planets and the set of things which are visible to the naked eye have an intersection, and that intersection contains exactly five elements. Similarly in the second sentence the intersection of two sets is claimed to have exactly 126 members, and so on for any numeral. Each numeral denotes a relation between sets such that the intersection contains the required number of objects.

EXERCISE ✎

7.6 Draw the Venn diagram for the first sentence of (7.5), with crosses representing the planets.

The denotation of the numeral five is thus a relation between sets – that is, all the ordered pairs of sets whose intersection has five elements. The set of planets and the set of visible objects is one such pair. So is the set of European nations and the set of rugby-playing nations (until Italy joins next year): and likewise the set of European states and the set of bits of former Yugoslavia. The relation denoted by 'five' comprises all such ordered pairs.

✎ **EXERCISE**

7.7   Draw Venn diagrams for the following sentences, and specify the conditions which the two sets must satisfy for the sentence to be true.

    a   All planes are fuelled.
    b   Four planes are fuelled.
    c   All four planes are fuelled.
    d   No planes are fuelled.
    e   At least one plane is not fuelled.
    f   All planes except one are fuelled.
    g   Most planes are fuelled.

All these quantifiers denote relations between sets (i.e. *ordered* pairs of sets). You may have noticed, however, that the ordering seems to matter more in some cases than in others. Let's see what happens if we reverse the order.

(7.8) 1   All politicians are rich (i.e. rich people).
        2   All rich people are politicians.

(7.9) 1   No Muslims drink alcohol.
        2   No drinkers of alcohol are Muslims.

(7.10) 1   Three million Londoners drink tea.
        2   Three million tea-drinkers are Londoners.

In the first case, reversing the order is disastrous – the two sentences mean different things. In the other cases the problem is not so obvious; the sentences imply each other, and thus have the same meaning (they are equivalent).[2] Nonetheless you might agree that in both cases the second sentence is a rather odd way of expressing it. In the next examples you can see one reason why.

(7.11)   All students were tired.

(7.12)   Some students were drunk.

(7.13)   No students were revising.

Which students are being talked about here? Plainly not all the students in the world. (In fact, the full denotation of 'students' would

include all the students who have ever existed or could ever exist –
a set about which one might hesitate to say anything very much.)
The sentences seem, rather, to refer to the students in a particular
situation, a group who can be readily picked out by the intended
hearer (or reader) of the sentence.

By contrast, the second set doesn't seem to have this effect. We
don't have to know anything about the whole set of tired entities,
drunk entities or revising entities in order to understand the sentence.

Thus when two sets are related by a quantifier they have different
roles. The first set establishes what entities we are talking about. It
restriction is known as the RESTRICTION set.

The second set is the main predicate of the sentence. Compare
these two sentences:

(7.14) 1   John was awake.
       2   No students were awake.

In both sentences the predicate is *awake*. In the first case the
sentence can be translated into predicate notation as *awake (john)*,
as will be familiar from Chapter 3. The predicate *awake* has the
same function in the second sentence, although this time it does not
have an individual as its argument. (We will shortly be looking at
ways of writing quantified sentences in predicate-argument notation.)
When we are dealing with quantifiers, this second set is known as
scope the SCOPE of the quantifier.

So if we treat quantifiers as relations between sets, then we have
three things: the quantifier itself, the restriction and the scope.

(7.15) 1   No students were awake.
       2   Quantifier: *no*. Restriction: set of *students*. Scope:
          set of *awake_entities*.

Often the sets denoted by common nouns can be restricted in
other ways as well. One is when the noun has an adjective with it.
If 'Skoda' denotes the set of *skodas*, then 'red Skoda' will denote a
subset of that, namely the set of *red_skodas*. You can see that this
subset is precisely the intersection of the set of skodas with the set
of red entities.

(7.16)

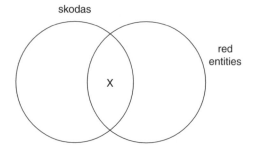

Being in the intersection of two sets like this corresponds to having both of the properties concerned. To say that an object (x in the diagram) is a red Skoda is equivalent to saying that it is a Skoda and it is a red entity. Not all adjectives can be treated in this way. It can only be done if the adjective-noun combination can be paraphrased in the way just described.

✐ EXERCISE

7.17 Which of the following combinations can be paraphrased in this way?

  a   honest politician
  b   big mouse
  c   former mistress
  d   green man
  e   good burglar

The set denoted by a noun may be similarly restricted by other expressions.

✐ EXERCISE

7.18 What are the sets picked out by the restricting expressions in square brackets? Draw Venn diagrams illustrating the intersection with the set denoted by the noun.

  a   houses [in London]
  b   girls [wearing bikinis]
  c   men [who snore]
  d   symphonies [which Mozart composed]
  e   students [who don't smoke]

7.1 SUMMARY

Often an argument is not a proper name but a quantifier, generally accompanied by a common noun. This chapter has suggested a treatment of quantifiers as relations between sets. Common nouns denote sets, exactly as they do when they occur as the main predicate of a sentence. The common noun accompanying a quantifier is called the restriction; it may be further restricted by certain kinds of adjectives or other expressions. The main predicate of the sentence is called the scope of the quantifier. The quantifier expresses a particular relation between its restriction and its scope.

What we cannot yet do is write sentences with quantifiers in the predicate-argument notation introduced in Chapter 3. In that chapter, only arguments which denote individuals were allowed. This question will be addressed in the next chapter.

7.2 SUPPLE-MENTARY EXERCISES ✎

7.19 Some quantifiers (like 'everybody') come with a 'built-in' restriction set (in this case the set of people). The denotation of 'every' was all the ordered pairs such that the first is a subset of the second. With 'everybody' we don't have to worry about the restriction set – so the denotation is simply all the sets of which the set of people is a subset.

a   Give two examples of such sets which will be part of the denotation of 'everybody'.

b   What will be the denotations of 'somebody' and 'nobody'? Again, give two examples of the denotation of each.

c   You can now answer the question posed at the beginning of the chapter. What is the difference between the denotations of 'nobody' and 'nothing'?

7.20 Quantifiers have an effect on entailment patterns. As with the lexical examples discussed in Chapter 4 (4.19), these can often be understood in terms of relations between sets. In each pair of sentences, which of the expressions in italics denotes the larger set? Which sentence entails which?

a   i   All sportsmen *run quickly*.
     ii   All sportsmen *run*.

b   i   At least five students *drink vodka*.
     ii   At least five students *drink*.

c   i   No directors are *poor students*.
     ii   No directors are *students*.

d   i   Five professors are *over 60*.
     ii   Five professors are *over 50*.

e   i   Few countries have *won the world cup at least three times*.
     ii   Few countries have *won the world cup at least twice*.

7.21 Under certain conditions in English, 'some' is replaced by 'any' (compare 'I have got some money' with 'Have you got any money?'). Study these sentences and suggest one of the relevant conditions.

a   All sportsmen have some money.
b   At least five students have some money.
c   No directors have any money.
d   Five professors have some money.
e   Few countries have any money.

1 More precisely, that the intersection is the empty set, whereas 'some' claim that it is a non-empty set.

2 The subset relation between sets is not symmetric, whereas the intersection relation is (cf. Chapter 10.1).

Notes

8 QUANTIFIERS (2)

In Chapter 3 predicates were introduced, but these were assumed to take individuals as their arguments (typically represented by proper names). In the previous chapter, in the course of discussing quantifiers, we looked at predicates whose arguments involved what are called 'common nouns' (such as 'student' or 'cricketer'). These can also be predicates ('John is a student') – but in these examples they showed up together with a quantifier (as in 'all students'), with another expression as the main predicate. They still denote a set (this time the restriction set for the quantifier). This chapter is going to extend some of these notions. First, it will look at ways of extending the predicate-argument notation so that its arguments can include these quantified expressions as well as individuals. (In fact we will look at two subtly different ways of doing this.)

Have another look at the Venn diagrams for the basic quantifiers *all, some* and *none*.

(8.1)

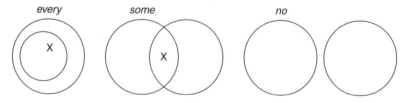

In these diagrams, crosses were used to mark the presence of individuals in sets. It didn't matter which individuals. We could discuss the relations involved without knowing the names of any Australians, or of any sportspeople. Effectively these crosses were playing the role of VARIABLES – something which can stand in for any individual.

variables

In the first diagram, suppose you can put a cross anywhere in the set of Australians. Wherever you put it, it is true that it will also be inside the set of sportspeople. This holds, in other words, regardless of the identity of x. It holds 'for all x'. The expression 'for all x' is usually abbreviated to '∀x' (the ∀ symbol is known as the UNIVER-SAL QUANTIFIER). So what the diagram is claiming is that 'for all x (assuming x is an Australian), x is a sportsperson'. We can now extend the notation introduced in Chapter 3 to include such statements:

universal quantifier

(8.2)   ∀x sportsperson(x)

In the second diagram, the important thing is that if you put crosses in the set of Australians, then it is possible to put one so that it is also in the set of sportspeople; whereas in the final diagram this is not possible, however hard you try. Thus in the second diagram the assertion 'x is a sportsperson' holds 'for some x' (equiv-alently, we can say that 'there is some x such that' the assertion holds). These expressions in quotation marks are usually abbrevi-ated to ∃x. the symbol ∃ is called the EXISTENTIAL QUANTIFIER.

existential quantifier

(8.3)   ∃x sportsperson(x)

In the last diagram there is no such x. So we can say that it is not true that there is an x for which the assertion holds.

(8.4)   ~∃x sportsperson(x)

Or equivalently, we can say that wherever you put an x, it will not be the case that the assertion holds (because it doesn't hold anywhere). This 'wherever you put an x' is the same condition that was used above for the universal quantifier, so the universal quan-tifier can be used here too.

(8.5)   ∀x ~(sportsperson(x))

✎ **EXERCISES**

8.6 Write the following as predicate-argument formulas. Assume that the variable x is restricted to humans.

a   Everybody is happy.
b   Somebody is snoring.
c   Nobody is singing.
d   Nobody likes Harry.
e   Maninder knows everybody.

8.7 What do the following mean in plain English? Again, assume x is restricted to humans.

a   ∃x clever(x)
b   ∀x asleep(x)
c   ~∃x know(x, bill)
d   ∃x kill(fagin, x)
e   ∀x ~forget(x. risa)

The restriction of x to humans is necessary, of course, because otherwise x would refer to any object in the universe, which is not what we want. It amounts to assuming that the restriction set for the quantifier is the set of *people*. We can make this explicit by writing the restriction after the quantifier:

(8.8)	**Quantifier**	**Restriction**	**Scope**
	$\forall x,$	person(x),	happy(x)

This can equally be done whatever other restriction is provided by the sentence (usually, of course, by the noun following the quantifier).

EXERCISE ✎

8.9 Translate these sentences into predicate notation, using quantifiers and variables.

    a   All dogs are smelly.
    b   Some politicians are honest.
    c   All children love Magda.
    d   No trains are late.
    e   John likes some animals.

There is an alternative way of dealing with restrictions. Look again at the diagrams in (8.1), and abandon the assumption that you can only put crosses inside the restriction set. Assume you can put crosses anywhere in the diagram you like. Then what can we say about these crosses?

In the first diagram, it is obvious that wherever we put a cross, it cannot be inside the set of Australians but outside the set of sportspeople. Thus for any x in the entire diagram, the following statement holds: 'if x is an Australian then x is a sportsperson'. In other words:

(8.10) $\forall x$ (australian(x) $\rightarrow$ sportsperson (x))

The outer brackets mark out the statement which is claimed to hold 'for all x'. There is no restriction on x.

In the second and third diagrams the question is whether we can put a cross (anywhere in the diagram) so that it is in both sets at once. In other words something which will answer to the descriptions 'australian' and 'sportsperson' at the same time. Clearly this is possible in the second but not in the third. In the second, it is true of some x that 'x is an Australian and a sportsperson':

(8.11) $\exists x$ (australian(x) & sportsperson(x))

In the third diagram there is no x for which this statement would hold:

(8.12) $\sim \exists x$ (australian(x) & sportsperson(x))

Or equivalently, wherever you put an *x*, this statement does not hold:

(8.13)   ∀x ~(australian(x) & sportsperson(x))

This approach, where variables are not restricted, is characteristic of a system called 'first order logic'. (The predicate-argument notation that you learnt in Chapter 3, together with the connectives in Chapter 2 and the treatment of quantifiers in the last few paragraphs, in fact forms the basis of first order logic.) You will meet both approaches in semantics, and it is best to become familiar with both of them.

🖉 **EXERCISES**

8.14   Translate the sentences of (8.9) into first order logic.

8.15   What do these expressions mean in plain English?

    a   ∃x (skoda(x) & work(x))
    b   ∀x (city(x) → dirty(x))
    c   ~∃x (professor(x) & smile(x))
    d   ∀x (student(x) → know(x, mary))
    e   ∀x ~(newspaper(x) & read(john, x))

The restrictions provided by adjectives etc. can also be incorporated into this notation quite straightforwardly. In the previous chapter it was seen that these are simply set intersections. These correspond to formulas linked by & (if *x* is in the intersection of two sets, then both the predicates truly describe *x*).

(8.16) 1   a   All red skodas work.
         b   ∀x ((skoda(x) & red(x)) → work(x))
      2   a   All girls who Nadia knows like Sasha.
         b   ∀x ((girl(x) & know(nadia, x)) → like(x, sasha))

8.1   Summary

This chapter has extended the predicate-argument notation to include quantifiers and variables. This enables sentences to be expressed in which the arguments are not simply individuals but may include common nouns, adjectives and even whole sentences.

One way of doing this (which was closer to the approach of the previous chapter) involved restricting the variable. This is not unlike what is seen in natural language, where quantifiers normally occur with common nouns which act as their restriction.

The second approach showed that it is possible to get rid of the restrictions and get the same effect by adding extra conditions to the main formula. (At least, this is possible for the quantifiers discussed in this chapter.) The complete notation, with quantifiers and variables, then corresponds to a well-known logical system called first order logic.

8.2 SUPPLEMENTARY EXERCISES ✎

8.17   Translate into first order predicate-argument formulas:

a   All crowded cities are dangerous.
b   Some intelligent students are rich.
c   No beautiful women like John.
d   No honest politicians are businessmen.
e   All useful books are interesting.

8.18   Translate into first order predicate-argument formulas:

a   All students who know John know Mary.
b   No students who like John like Mary.
c   Some tourists who visit London are rich.
d   All dishes which Anili cooks are delicious.
e   Some students who drink tequila dance.

8.19   To express the meaning of 'all' in first order logic, two predicates are used, linked by the → sign: $\forall x\ (P(x) \rightarrow Q(x))$. For 'some', the two predicates were linked by the & sign: $\exists x\ (P(x)\ \&\ Q(x))$. Why must these particular connectives be used? Consider the following expressions, and state what they would mean.

a $\forall x$ (australian(x) & sportsperson(x))
b $\exists x$ (australian(x) → sportsperson(x))

8.20   To express the meaning of 'none', two alternative formulas were given. One involved using $\forall x$, the other $\exists x$. In fact this is a general principle, that anything that can be expressed using one quantifier can be expressed using the other, simply by judicious use of negation. If an assertion is true 'for all x', then there is no x for which it is false. Conversely if it is true 'for some x', then it is not the case that it is false for all x. Re-express each of these formulas using the other quantifier.

a $\forall x$ (australian(x) → sportsperson(x))
b $\exists x$ (australian(x) & sportsperson(x))

ARGUMENT STRUCTURE

9

The predicate plays a central part in determining what other elements can occur in a sentence. Earlier chapters have examined two ways in which it does this. First it denotes a relation which assigns roles, and the entities filling these roles will show up in the sentence as arguments. (In the last couple of chapters this was generalized so that arguments need no longer be particular individuals.) In Chapter 6 it was seen that predicates may denote different types of event or state, and this interacts in important ways both with the arguments and with other elements in the sentence.

This final chapter will take another look at the part played by the *meaning* of a predicate in determining what arguments it has, and hence the structure of the sentence.

Consider what is probably the simplest kind of argument structure, that required by a simple predicate like 'is a student' or 'is a dolphin'. These can be used to classify individuals in the world. The argument of such a predicate can be described as an INSTANCE – an instantiation of the property denoted by the predicate. This should be familiar from Chapter 5.

Now look at this slightly more complicated case. Imagine a crowd outside a football stadium. You could describe them all as 'fans', but it would be apparent that this is not a property that unites them. They would be likely to insist on the importance of a certain distinction between (say) Arsenal fans and Tottenham fans. The difference depends entirely on the difference between the football teams in question. Thus the predicate 'is a fan' is not a simple property, but a relation between an individual and another entity (in this case a football team). It would be more correct to write it not as *fan(x)* but rather as *fan_of(x. y)*, where *y* is a team. This extra 'of' often appears after nouns or adjectives to indicate the presence of an extra argument.

instance

EXERCISE

9.1 The second arguments of these predicates (in italics) are not expressed, but they still invite the question 'Of what?' (or 'Of whom?'). Suggest plausible candidates for the second argument.

a   'Congratulations on becoming a *father*.'
b   'Ignore her. She's only *jealous*.'
c   'Don't shoot! He's a *friend*.'
d   '*Buyers* beware.'
e   'That puzzle is a real *teaser*.'

In these examples the 'of' is optional. This is normally the case for nouns and adjectives in English.[1]

Besides categorizing an individual, a one-place predicate may describe a situation in which an entity finds itself – perhaps temporarily (cf. Chapter 6). A good example is location. However, location is like the predicates in (9.1), in that it requires another expression to fix the location of the entity, i.e. another argument. Often that involves an already familiar object which serves as a 'reference point'. (Location is usually fixed relative to some comparatively stable object in the environment, rather than in absolute terms. For example it would be more normal to say 'John is in Cambridge' than to give his latitude and longitude.) Where exactly the entity is in relation to the reference point is usually expressed (in English) by a preposition (words like 'in' or 'under'). Because this describes a relation, it can be considered a predicate.

(9.2) 1   a   John is in Cambridge.
          b   in(john, cambridge)

      2   a   John is under the table.
          b   under(john, the_table)

theme   From now on the entity being located (*john* in the examples) will be referred to as the THEME. (Warning: this term is used in a variety of senses in different linguistic theories.)

EXERCISE

9.3 Identify the theme and the reference point(s) in the following sentences. Why does the second sentence of each pair sound odd?

a   i   The airliner was near the runway.
    ii   The runway was near the airliner.

b   i   There was a flag over the building.
    ii   There was a building under the flag.

c   i   The girl was inside the forest.
    ii   The forest was around the girl.

The spatial relations used so far have been stative (Chapter 6). However, similar relations can be used to express events; for example *change* of location. Once again a reference object is often used. The preposition in this case combines with the reference object to describe the path which the theme follows.

(9.4) 1   The plane flew *to* Moscow.
     2   The plane flew *towards* Moscow.
     3   The train came *into* the station.
     4   The train went *out of* the station.
     5   John walked *towards* Mary's house.
     6   John walked *away from* Mary's house.
     7   John walked *from* Mary's house *to* Sarah's house.

✎ **EXERCISES**

9.5 The paths described in the above sentences can each be described as a line (not necessarily straight) with a particular location at one or both ends.

    a   In which sentences is that location *included* in the path followed by the theme?
    b   Which sentences describe telic events?

9.6 Some of these paths can be combined with the verb of movement into a single verb. Match each of these verbs with a sentence in (9.4).

    enter   approach   reach   leave

Which of the verbs describe telic events?

Much the same structures that are used to express change of location can be used to describe change of state in general, for example when we are dealing with temporary properties (like drunkenness, cf. Chapter 6), or possession.

(9.7) 1   a   Mary was in John's study.
        b   Mary went to the gym.
        c   John stayed in his study.

     2   a   John *was* in a bad mood.
        b   John's face *went* from sad to angry.
        c   Mary *stayed* calm.

     3   a   The house *was* John's.
        b   After the settlement the house *went* to Mary.
        c   The overdraft *stayed* with John.

This appears to reflect the central role played by spatial location and movement in the way the human mind organizes information.

So far we have looked at some of the typical argument structures associated with nouns, adjectives and prepositions in English. The argument structures of verbs are often more complicated.

EXERCISE

9.8   What are the arguments of these sentences? Which arguments could you leave out?

a   'Mary devoured her pizza.'
b   'Mary ate her pizza.'
c   'Sarah cleared the table of plates.'
d   'Sarah cleared the plates from the table.'
e   'John handed Mary a vase.'
f   'John bought Mary a vase.'

It is clear from this exercise that not only do verbs with apparently similar meanings differ in their argument requirements, but 'the same' verb may appear in different patterns with different requirements. The syntactic form of a sentence reflects these requirements, which are known as the verb's argument structure. (This argument structure is said to be 'projected' into the syntax.) This is an important but complicated part of the relationship (or 'interface') between semantics and syntax. The following sections can only look at a few of the simpler patterns.

(9.9)   1   Dante wrote *The Divine Comedy*.
        2   *The Divine Comedy* was written by Dante.

The sentences, first of all, describe the same event – a writing event, with two roles. In the first sentence, the first argument (the SUBJECT) refers to the filler of the *writer* role, while the noun immediately after the verb (the direct OBJECT) refers to the *thing written*.[2] In the second sentence the latter has become the subject; while the *writer* is introduced by 'by' (another preposition). Many verbs which have two or more arguments can appear in both of these patterns.

subject
object

It is important to be clear that subject and object are syntactic terms, not semantic ones. This should be apparent from the examples in (9.9). The subject and object change, while the meaning of the sentences remains essentially the same: *write (dante, the_divine_comedy)*. The subject (and the object if there is one) can be thought of as slots in the sentence which have to be filled by appropriate *expressions*; in the notation we have been using, the subject of the first sentence is 'Dante', not *dante*. At the semantic level the relation denoted by the verb assigns the *writer* role to the entity *dante* (in both sentences). The study of argument structure is concerned with how these apparently separate requirements are linked – so that the verb does not, for example, have 'Dante' as its subject but then assign *dante* the role of the thing written.

9.10 Pick out the subject and object of the first four sentences in (9.8) above. Which roles are assigned to which entities?

9.11 Do the same for the following sentences, in which the verbs are 'nonsense words'. Who do you think is 'doing something' to whom?

    a   Maria frickled Angelica.
    b   The students shodded the director of research.
    c   The hedgehog tarked the farmer.

Your (probable) reaction to the last exercise shows that the pattern in which the subject denotes an entity responsible for an action and the object an entity affected by it is a natural one, which seems to be expected by a language user. In fact this particular way of linking semantic roles with syntactic structure is prevalent in most languages (and is also something that children are sensitive to at an early stage). This is true even though in fact it is not always the case that a verb represents an action done by one entity to another (it may not even denote an action at all).

9.12 In which cases is the referent of the object affected by the action described?

    a   The dragon ate *Maria* for breakfast.
    b   The builders saw *Rachel* walking down the road.
    c   Mary pushed *Jane* over the edge.
    d   The lifeboat brought *Peter* to the shore.
    e   Many people admire *Napoleon*.

A particular case of an 'affected object' is one whose referent undergoes a change of state (which includes, as usual, change of location). Such entities are of interest because they can be expressed either by a subject or by an object, under certain conditions.

In (9.4) above, the theme was (the referent of) the subject of the sentence. However it can equally well be the object. Compare the following sentences:

(9.13) 1 The hijackers flew *the plane* to Moscow.
 2 The robbers lured *the train* into the station.
 3 Despair drove *John* from Mary's house to Sarah's house.

In these cases the theme is now expressed by the object, while the subject has introduced another entity which acts as the *cause* of the event. Note that in each case the new sentence *entails* the corresponding sentence in (9.4), where the theme appeared as subject, and also entails that this event was *caused* by the referent of the new subject.

EXERCISE ✎

9.14 Find pairs of verbs which have senses related in the same way.

come   drop   take   bring   kill   fall
die   go

There are a number of verbs which can appear with two different argument patterns, one including the cause and one not. In other words the same word has two senses, systematically related in the way just described. This has a strong tendency to occur with change of state verbs (though things are not always as neat and tidy as that).

(9.15) 1 a The window broke.
 b The cricket ball broke the window.

 2 a The ice melted.
 b The greenhouse gases melted the ice.

One final case involving change of state occurs when the movement of the theme may have an effect on the 'reference object' in the background. If this is construed as the most important effect of the event, then the latter, rather than the theme, may be expressed as the object of the sentence.

(9.16) 1 a The farmers sprayed pesticide onto the field.
 b The farmers sprayed the field with pesticide.

 2 a Tina injected vodka and tabasco into the tomatoes.
 b Tina injected the tomatoes with vodka and tabasco.

EXERCISE ✎

9.17 In each of the above sentences identify the theme and the object. Which form of the sentences would you expect to be used if

a   Only a little of the substance(s) had been applied.
b   The fields were now an ecological hazard.
c   The tomatoes were liable to make you drunk?

9.18 How would you account for the fact that the following verbs do not allow both patterns?

   a   i   The waitress poured wine into the glass.
       ii * The waitress poured the glass with wine.

   b   i   * The waitress filled wine into the glass.
       ii The waitress filled the glass with wine.

Phenomena like these are useful because they show which aspects of the meaning of a verb are linguistically important (in other words make a systematic difference to the way the events can be expressed in language).

This section has given an introduction to the way that the meaning of a predicate determines its argument structure, and hence affects the syntactic structure of sentences in which it occurs. It is important to keep the syntactic and semantic aspects of argument structure distinct, in order to study how they are linked.

    Some features which bear on this question have been introduced, following some of the main lines of recent research. Predicates often involve the categorization of entities, which may or may not involve a relation with other entities. They may also express temporary states, particularly important examples of which include location and change of location. The patterns associated with verbs also reflect the idea of an action having an entity responsible for causing it, and of a specifiable effect on other entities. These recurring ideas (along with others which have been omitted here) also play a central role in the study of human cognition, and it has been suggested that the way they underpin the structure of language shows an intimate connection between natural language and other cognitive faculties.

9.1   Summary

1   There are a few exceptions, like 'fond'.
2   This rough-and-ready way of identifying them applies specifically to English, which has a characteristic *Subject Verb Object* word order in basic sentences.

Notes

10 APPENDICES

One way of approaching sets is to think of them as arranging things (INDIVIDUALS) by putting them into boxes. The box is called a set and the things inside it are the ELEMENTS of the set.

By convention, sets are labelled with capital letters and individuals with lower case letters. The symbol $\in$ stands for the *element_of* relation, so that if an individual a is an element of a set S, this can be written '$a \in$ S'. For example if Irina belongs to the set of supermodels, this can be written '*irina* $\in$ Supermodels'.

Some boxes may contain a completely haphazard collection of items, others may have been packed in some more organized way. In the first case the contents can be simply listed. Thus if the set S consists of the elements a, b and c, then we can write 'S = {a, b, c}'. The order is not important, so if we have a set {b c, a} then it is the same set. (However it is important that no element should be listed twice.) For more organized sets, it is sufficient to state a rule determining what goes inside it, like putting a label on the box. Such rules are often written using the symbol '|' or ':' to mean 'such that'. If S consists of all red objects, then S = {x | red(x)} ('the set of all x such that x is red').

Note that a box may contain a smaller box. In this case a small box is treated as an element of the set. But its contents are not; they are only elements of the smaller set represented by the small box. When listing the elements of the larger set, it is assumed that we have just taken the lid off the large box, and cannot see inside the smaller one.

Supposing S is a set of countries, {italy, uzbekistan, {england, scotland}, japan}. The small set {england, scotland} counts as one element, and for the purposes of the larger set you cannot see inside it. Let's say that being an element of the larger set represents having a vote in some international body, and England and Scotland have one vote between them.

The one thing you can't do (in standard set theory) is make a set a member of itself. If you think in terms of boxes, you will not be tempted to do so.

It is assumed that all the individuals we are concerned with are already elements of a big set – precisely 'the set of all individuals'. This is known as 'the UNIVERSAL SET' (U) or 'the DOMAIN OF DISCOURSE' (D).

There is also a set containing nothing at all – the NULL or EMPTY set. You can imagine several boxes all containing nothing, but remember that if two sets have exactly the same elements then they are the same set, and this applies here too. The empty set can be written { } to indicate a set with nothing inside it, but it is normally given the special symbol ∅.

A set containing exactly one element is called a SINGLETON set.

10.1.2   Some special sets

universal set
domain of discourse
null
empty

singleton

A subset of S is another set formed using elements of S *and nothing else*; intuitively, another box into which we can put as many elements of S as we like. If S = {a, b, c} as above, then the set {a, b} is a subset of S. So is the set {a, c}, and so is the singleton set {b} (for example). We can include all the elements, or none at all if we like. Thus S is a subset of itself, and the empty set ∅ is also a subset of S. The only restriction is that we cannot include anything as an element which is not an element of S.

Although this looks simple, it is easy to confuse elements and subsets. For S as specified, the only *elements* are *a*, *b* and *c*, while *subsets* are new sets formed from any selection of these elements (or all or none of them). The main source of confusion is the fact that sets can be elements of sets, as described above. Suppose we have a set T = {a, b, {c, d}, e}. This has four elements (not five), one of which is set {c, d}. The latter is an *element* of T, but not a *subset*. A subset of T will be a set which may include {c, d} as one of its elements. In the simplest case this will be the singleton set {{c, d}}. The little box {c, d} has been taken from T and put in the new box which is the subset.

10.1.3   Subsets

(10.1)   List all the subsets of the following sets:

a   {a, b, c}
b   {a, {b, c}}
c   {a}
d   {a, b, { }, c}

The subsets of a set S are all possible combinations of the elements of S; this includes S itself and the empty set. It a set has n elements, then it has 2^n subsets. You can check this against your answers to (10.1).

The subset relation is written '⊆'; A ⊆ S means 'A is a subset of S'. (Conversely S is a SUPERSET of A, sometimes written S ⊇ A.)

superset

proper subset

This relation includes the possibility that the two are equal, as explained. If we want to specify a subset of S which does not contain *all* the elements of S, we can call it a PROPER SUBSET, and write A ⊂ S (or S ⊃ A).

(10.2)   What is the relation (if any) between the sets A and B in each of these examples?

a   A = {a, b, c}; B = {a, b, c, d}
b   A = {a, b, { }}; B = {a, b}
c   A = {a, b, c}; B = {a, {b, c}}

10.1.4 Set operations

Sets can be combined to form new sets. The following are the three most important operations.

complement

If S is a set, then you can form the set of all individuals which are *not* elements of S. This is the COMPLEMENT of S. A slightly more restricted notion is the set of all elements of some set T which are not elements of S. This can be termed 'the complement of S in T' (or T – S). Of course the *unrestricted* notion of complement can be thought of as 'the complement of S in U' (U – S).

union

intersection

If there are two sets S and T, then the UNION of S and T (S ∪ T) is the set containing all the elements of S and all the elements of T (and nothing else). The INTERSECTION of S and T (S ∩ T) is the set containing all elements of S which are also elements of T. Thus if S = {john, mary, fred} and T = {bill, mary, fred, jane}, then S ∩ T will be {mary, fred} and S ∪ T will be {john, mary, fred, bill, jane}. (Remember that the result is a set, so every element in it is only counted once.)

10.1.5 Relations

A relation is a kind of set, except that its elements are not normally single individuals but ordered listings of a specified size. Each relation specifies whether it is to hold between two elements, three elements or whatever. For a two-place (or 'binary') relation the size specified is two, and the elements of the relation will therefore be ORDERED PAIRS.

ordered pairs

As an intuitive example, imagine we have a set of people and we want to record who loves whom. Then *love* is a binary relation, whose elements are pairs of individuals such that the first one loves the second one. The ordering is important, because obviously if *a* loves *b*, there is no guarantee that *b* loves *a*. Also note that there is no restriction that *a* has to love only one person, or that the person loved has to be someone distinct from *a*.

In this example both members of the ordered pair were restricted to people (they were taken from the same set). Equally we may want to impose different restrictions; for example for the relation *write*, the first member of each ordered pair will be taken from the set of people (P) and the second from the set of books (B).

It may help to think of this relation as a chart with elements of P listed horizontally and elements of B listed vertically. That gives you a 'space', or grid, from which particular cells can be 'ticked off' if the relation in question does actually hold for them. The 'space' can be referred to as P × B, and the relation *write* will denote a subset of P × B, namely those cells which are ticked off.

If the two sets are the same (as in the *love* example), then imagine a similar grid with people listed both horizontally and vertically. (The relation is then a subset of P × P.)

The complement of a relation is the set of those ordered pairs which are not elements of the relation (i.e. the cells which are not ticked). Thus the complement of *love* is those ordered pairs in P × P of which the *love* relation does not hold.

Some types of binary relations are singled out for special properties which make them useful.

A REFLEXIVE relation is one which holds between an individual and itself.

A SYMMETRIC relation is one which, if we know that it holds between two individuals in one direction, then we know that it holds for the same two individuals in the reverse direction as well. An example would be the *going_out_with* relation. Unlike the *love* relation, which allows the possibility of unrequited love, if you are going out with somebody then they are going out with you.

A TRANSITIVE relation is one which, if it holds between x and y, and also between y and z, must also hold between x and z. An example is the *taller_than* relation. If John is taller than Mary and Mary is taller than Fred, then John must be taller than Fred.

10.1.6   Some special types of binary relation

reflexive
symmetric

transitive

Functions are another special kind of binary relation. They are not used much in this book, but are of great importance in semantics in general. Remember with the *love* relation there was no restriction that everybody has to love only one person (nor for that matter that they have to love anybody at all). Compare this with the idea of having a father. Each person has one (biological) father, and only one. This is a FUNCTION – a relation that associates each individual in one set with one and only one individual in another set.[1]

Although functions are a kind of relation, they are normally given a different notation. The information that Fred's father is Bill, for example, will be written: 'father_of(fred) = bill'. In this example *father_of* is the function, *fred* is an argument and *bill* is the value of the function (for that argument).

The set from which the arguments are taken is the domain of a function and the set from which the values are taken is its range. The *father_of* function has (let's say) the set of humans as its domain and the set of men as its range. It is function from the set of humans into the set of men.

Some of the ideas in this book are often formalized as functions. Here are a few examples.

10.1.7 Functions

function

(10.3) 1   Under the assumptions we have been using, each statement has one and only one truth value. Thus there is a function from the set of statements to the set of truth values (the latter being a small set: {*true, false*}). In fact each 'window' (Chapter 2) is, formally speaking, just such a function; it tells you whether a given statement has the value *true* or *false*.

2   If each proper name denotes a particular individual, and each predicate denotes a set, then this can be treated as a function from the set of basic expressions in a language to a universal set or domain of discourse.

3   The connectives in Chapter 2 can be regarded as functions from truth values to truth values. If you give them a combination of truth values (a row in the truth table), they will give you a truth value which is the result.

4   A one-place predicate (or property) combines with its argument to give either a true statement or a false statement. Thus *american(bill_clinton) = true*, while *american(boris_yeltsin) = false*. Such a predicate is a function from individuals to truth values.

5   If the predicate has a second argument, then it combines with it to give a property. Thus *fan_of* combines with Arsenal to give the property of being an Arsenal fan, while it combines with Tottenham to give the very different property of being a Tottenham fan (Chapter 9). In other words it is a function from individual entities (in this case teams) to properties.

6   The quantifiers in Chapter 7 combine with the restriction set to give all the sets which stand in particular relation to it. Thus *every* combines with the set *Dogs* to give all the supersets of *Dogs*, while it combines with *Students* to give all the supersets of *Students*. Thus these quantifiers can be treated as functions from sets to 'sets of sets'.

10.4   There are certain advantages to treating things in this way, using functions. However, consider the first two examples and see if you can spot some obvious drawbacks. (It may help to look back at Chapter 1 and the beginning of Chapter 2.)

1.1 a   The interpretation of a word in a language (possibly via its equivalent in a known language).
   b   Intending a particular action or result.
   c   Somebody has presumably suggested that the speaker has said something that does not correspond with what he really thinks, or intended to communicate.
   d   To imply – to enable us to draw a conclusion.
   e   Again to imply, this time on the basis of a stereotype suggested by a word.
   f   This is a tricky one, because what is really being contrasted is two kinds of *meaning* – the literal meaning of the words used (as in example 1) against what the hearer is intended to understand.

10.2   KEY TO EXERCISES

**CHAPTER 1
Pinning down semantics**

1.2 *lies = porkies; bottle = guts$_1$; guts$_2$ = intestines; gift = present$_1$; present$_2$ = current; shop$_1$ = store$_1$; shop$_2$ = betray; store$_2$ = hoard*

1.5 1   Einstein College / its
   2   the director / him (twice) / his
   3   the chairman / he
   4   students / their / they
   5   residence / accommodation
   6   representative / Tracy Sharpe

1.7 (Sample answer)
   a   'Bank'. Sense 1 (*bank$_1$*), the financial organization, has a denotation including: the bank of england, nat west, etc. 'The pound has fallen again, so [the bank] will have to adjust interest rates'. Reference: the bank of england
      Sense 2 (*bank$_2$*), the edge of a river, has a denotation including: the bank of the thames, the bank of the jordan, etc.
      'Between here and the Jordan is heavily mined, so you need a guide to get to [the bank].' Reference: the bank of the jordan
   c   'Pig'. Sense 1 (*pig$_1$*), the animal with the curly tail, has a denotation including: piglet, napoleon, babe, etc.
      '"It's a good job [that pig] doesn't like honey", said Pooh.' Reference: piglet
      Sense 2 (*pig$_2$*), a person who eats too much, has a denotation including the emperor vitellius, henry viii, etc. Reference: you can make your own examples.

1.8 There are sixteen tokens, but only thirteen types. (The word-type 'the' has two tokens, and 'of' has three.)

1.9   Seven tokens, five types. The reference of 'I' and 'you' (and hence 'my' and 'your') changes when the same sentence type is used by different speakers.

1.10 a   No. Individuals as such cannot be true or false, they're just 'there'.

b   Yes.

c   Only if it is used as a sentence, with something like 'This is . . .' understood. Not if it is part of a phrase like 'a very nice wine'.

d   No. This phrase on its own doesn't say anything that could be evaluated as true or false.

e   Yes. It can be true that something is false.

f   No. The subphrase *they didn't come* can be true (and the speaker assumes that it is). But *the fact that they didn't come* simply refers to this assumed truth, it doesn't assert it. In other words it does not give it a truth value.

CHAPTER 2
Truth conditions

2.1 2 a   is difficult because 'quiet' is a relative term. Central London in the afternoon is quiet compared to Athens, but not compared to an examination room. (See Chapter 4.)

b   is another relative term, and also has an element of subjectivity.

c   is a statement which is not decided one way or the other by the current window; the information simply isn't there.

2.4   row 1: it is raining and it is cold
row 2: it is training but it is not cold
row 3: it is not raining but it is cold
row 4: it is neither raining nor cold

2.8 P = Michael Owen is injured
Q = Michael Owen is suspended

P	Q	$P \vee Q$
t	t	t
t	f	t
f	t	t
f	f	f

'Or' joins two or more statements to form a composite statement whose truth value is *true* if any of the component statements are *true*; otherwise it is *false*.

2.9 a P = the boat capsized
Q = John fell in

P	Q	$P \vee Q$
t	t	t
t	f	t
f	t	t
f	f	f

b P = Chelsea won
Q = West Ham drew
R = Arsenal lost

P	Q	R	$P \& Q$	$(P \& Q) \vee R$
t	t	t	t	t
t	t	f	t	t
t	f	t	f	t
t	f	f	f	f
f	t	t	f	t
f	t	f	f	f
f	f	t	f	t
f	f	f	f	f

c P = Pooh will have honey
Q = Pooh will have maple syrup
R = Pooh will have clotted cream

P	Q	R	$Q \vee R$	$P \& (Q \vee R)$
t	t	t	t	t
t	t	f	t	t
t	f	t	t	t
t	f	f	f	f
f	t	t	t	f
f	t	f	t	f
f	f	t	t	f
f	f	f	f	f

2.11 The two meanings can be expressed as:

1 Either John paid Mary and Mary paid Bill, or John paid Bill.
2 John paid Mary, and either John paid Bill or Mary paid Bill.

2.13

1	P	Q	R	P & Q	(P & Q) ∨ R
	t	t	t	t	t
	t	t	f	t	t
	t	f	t	f	t
	t	f	f	f	f
	f	t	t	f	t
	f	t	f	f	f
	f	f	t	f	t
	f	f	f	f	f

2	P	Q	R	Q ∨ R	P & (Q ∨ R)
	t	t	t	t	t
	t	t	f	t	t
	t	f	t	t	t
	t	f	f	f	f
	f	t	t	t	f
	f	t	f	t	f
	f	f	t	t	f
	f	f	f	f	f

2.16

P	Q	~P	~Q	~P ∨ ~Q
t	t	f	f	f
t	f	f	t	t
f	t	t	f	t
f	f	t	t	t

2.20   P = she passed the exam

P	~P	P ∨ ~P
t	f	t
f	t	t

2.21

a   P = John proposed to Mary
Q = Mary hit John
R = John banged his head

(i)

P	Q	R	Q ∨ R	P & (Q ∨ R)
t	t	t	t	t
t	t	f	t	t
t	f	t	t	t
t	f	f	f	f
f	t	t	t	f
f	t	f	t	f

f	f	t	t	f
f	f	f	f	f

(ii)

P	Q	R	$P \& Q$	$P \& R$	$(P \& Q) \lor (P \& R)$
t	t	t	t	t	t
t	t	f	t	f	t
t	f	t	f	t	t
t	f	f	f	f	f
f	t	t	f	f	f
f	t	f	f	f	f
f	f	t	f	f	f
f	f	f	f	f	f

b P = Colonel Mustard did it
  Q = it was done in the billiards room
  R = it was done with the candlestick

(i)

P	Q	R	$Q \& R$	$P \lor (Q \& R)$
t	t	t	t	t
t	t	f	f	t
t	f	t	f	t
t	f	f	f	t
f	t	t	t	t
f	t	f	f	f
f	f	t	f	f
f	f	f	f	f

(ii)

P	Q	R	$P \lor Q$	$P \lor R$	$(P \lor Q) \& (P \lor R)$
t	t	t	t	t	t
t	t	f	t	t	t
t	f	t	t	t	t
t	f	f	t	t	t
f	t	t	t	t	t
f	t	f	t	f	f
f	f	t	f	t	f
f	f	f	f	f	f

2.22 The sentence has sixteen rows. In general if you have n statements, you will need 2^n rows. This makes truth tables for more than three statements very cumbersome. Fortunately there are much neater methods for determining the truth of such complex sentences, though you won't need to learn them here.

2.23 The truth conditions do not change – to all intents and purposes *and* is truth-conditionally equivalent to *but*. Since intuitively the sentences seem to convey different meanings, this is one well-known example where truth conditions appear to be inadequate by themselves.

2.24 It indicates that the truth conditions for & as defined in this chapter are not identical with the meaning of the English word 'and' (or its equivalent in many other languages). In particular they are inadequate when 'and' is used to connect statements describing a sequence of events. This will be further discussed in Chapter 6.

2.25

P	Q	$P \lor Q$	$P \& Q$	$\sim(P \& Q)$	$(P \lor Q) \& \sim(P \& Q)$
t	t	t	t	f	f
t	f	t	f	t	t
f	t	t	f	t	t
f	f	f	f	t	f

We could define a new symbol for 'exclusive or' – say X, so that 'P X Q' gives the values shown in the last column. In principle we can define in this way any connective we think will be useful. (See Chapter 4 for some more examples.) In practice 'inclusive or' is considered more useful – though not necessarily as an equivalent to the English word 'or'.

CHAPTER 3
Getting inside sentences

3.3

	Expression	Relation	No. of individuals
a	'has eaten'	*eat*	2
b	'was sent'	*send*	3
c	'stole'	*steal*	3
d	'is bigger than'	*bigger_than*	2
e	'goes round'	*go_round*	2

3.5 The role descriptions given here are only one among many possible answers:

a *eat* requires (i) an eater and (ii) the thing eaten.

b *send* requires (i) a sender, (ii) the thing (or person) sent, and (iii) a destination.

c *steal* requires (i) a thief, (ii) the object stolen, and (iii) a victim of the theft.

d *bigger_than* requires (i) a larger object and (ii) a smaller object.

e *go_round* requires (i) an orbiting object and (ii) a centre around which it moves.

3.8 a exciting(hawaii)
   b genius(plato)
   c admire(john, bill)
   d admire(bill, john)
   e taller_than(james, tina)
   f bark(cerberus)

3.9 a 'Bill is crazy.'
   b 'Gertrude is learning Latin' or 'Gertrude learnt Latin,' etc.
   c 'John gave the flowers to Lindsay,' etc.
   d 'Richard is the father of Henry,' etc.
   e '9 is the square of 3.'
   f 'Boris plays chess,' etc.

3.10 a The relation *want* holds of the ordered pairs <john, beer>, <bill, cider>, <mary, gin>, <sarah, lemonade>, <sebastian, sherry>.
   b The relation *study* holds of the ordered pairs <maria, turkish>, <ali, chinese>, <suresh, hausa>, <noriko, indonesian>, <natasha, arabic>.

3.11 The relation *kill* denotes the set whose members are the ordered pairs *<brutus, caesar>, <david, goliath>, <elizabeth_i, mary_queen_of_scots>, <henry_viii, thomas_more>, <henry_viii, ann_boleyn>*, and *<henry_viii, catherine_howard>*.

3.12 a The relation is *fall*. This only has one role – namely the person or thing which changes location (*Bill's sister*).
   b The relation is *talk*. It requires a speaker, and perhaps also a listener. However, the speaking role has to be filled by something which is human, or at least endowed with enough intelligence to use language.
   c The relation is *sell*. A selling situation requires a seller, a buyer and something to change hands. (Incidentally so does a *buying* situation, though the role players are arranged differently in the sentence.)
   d The relation is *give*. It requires a giver, a gift and a recipient. It is a fact about the English verb 'give' that normally all three roles have to be expressed; in particular you can't get away with leaving out the *gift*.
   e The relation is *drink*. Like eating situations, drinking requires a drinker and something suitable for drinking. The drinker has to be a person, not just a part of person. This illustrates the difference between the role require-

ments actually imposed by a verb and a purely scientific view of a situation.

f   The relationship is *rain*. Again it does not assign a role to *the umbrella*, even though umbrellas are often seen in raining situations. In fact the verb 'rain' is unusual in that it does not seem to assign any roles at all; 'it is raining' can be given a truth value as it stands, and it doesn't make sense to ask 'what is raining?'.

3.13 a   secretary(jill)
b   write(shakespeare, hamlet)
c   leak(the_minister, the_document, the_daily_stirrer)
d   think(sheila, irresponsible(bill))
e   tell(bruce, maria, think(ruth, steal(maria, nick, ruth)))

3.14 a   'Sheila is bossy.'
b   'New Delhi is the capital of India.'
c   'Ethiopia is in Africa.'
d   'The Falkland Islands are near Argentina.'
e   'John sent his mother-in-law to Australia.'

3.15 a   warmer_than(spain, england)
true – unless today's weather bulletins say otherwise
b   planet(mars) & ~planet(jupiter)
false
c   mother_of(queen_elizabeth, prince_charles) & footballer(prince_charles)
false
d   ~(north_of(italy, norway) ∨ american(gorbachev))
true

3.16 a   *russian* denotes the set {gagarin, kasparov}
woman denotes the set {thatcher, monroe}
kill denotes the set {<oswald, kennedy>, <monroe, monroe>}
lover_of denotes the set {<kennedy, monroe>, <monroe, kennedy>}
(You may wish to assume a different version of history.)
b   (i)   russian(kasparov) – *true*
(ii)   lover_of(gagarin, thatcher) – *false*
(iii)   woman(kennedy) – *false*
c   (i)   Make the denotation of 'Russian' a set which excludes the individual denotes by 'Kasparov'.
(ii)   Include the ordered pair <gagarin, thatcher> in the *lover_of* relation.

(iii) Include the individual *kennedy* in the set denoted by 'woman'.

4.4   1   The expression we need to evaluate is ~(P & ~Q)

P	Q	~Q	P & ~Q	~(P & ~Q)
t	t	f	f	t
t	f	t	t	f
f	t	f	f	t
f	f	t	f	t

2   The expression is ~P ∨ Q

P	Q	~P	~P ∨ Q
t	t	f	t
t	f	f	f
f	t	t	t
f	f	t	t

4.6   1   The expression is (P → Q) & (Q → P)

P	Q	P → Q	Q → P	(P → Q) & (Q → P)
t	t	t	t	t
t	f	f	t	f
f	t	t	f	f
f	f	t	t	t

The expression is only true in rows one and four, i.e. when both P and Q are true or when they are both false. The last column gives the truth conditions for P ≡ Q (or P ↔ Q).

2   The expression is (P → ~Q) & (Q → ~P)

P	Q	~P	~Q	P → ~Q	Q → ~P	(P → ~Q) & (Q → ~P)
t	t	f	f	f	f	f
t	f	f	t	t	t	t
f	t	t	f	t	t	t
f	f	t	t	t	t	t

The expression excludes just the case where P and Q are both true (row 1). They can both be false (row 4).

3   The expression is (P ≡ ~Q). The truth values for P ≡ Q are given by the final column in 1.

P	Q	~Q	P ≡ ~Q
t	t	f	f
t	f	t	t
f	t	f	t
f	f	t	f

This time the expression is true in rows two and three – i.e. if the truth values for P and Q are different. You can easily see that we could have got the same result using (Q ≡ ~P).

4.9   a   *crimson* is a hyponym of *red*. The set of crimson objects is a subset of the set of red objects.

b   *slap* is a hyponym of *hit*. The set of ordered pairs of which the relation *slap* holds is a subset of the set of ordered pairs of which the relation *hit* holds.

c   *lurch* is a hyponym of *walk*. The set of entities which lurch is a subset of the set of entities which walk. (This gets more complicated when metaphorical extensions of meaning are included – ships can naturally be described as 'lurching' but not as 'walking'.)

d   *shred* is a hyponym of *cut up*. The set of ordered pairs of which the relation *shred* holds is a subset of the set of ordered pairs of which the relation *cut up* holds.

e   *hand* is a hyponym of *give*. The set of ordered triples of which the relation *hand* holds is a subset of the set of ordered triples of which the relation *give* holds.

4.16   a   Contradictory antonyms, at least as I personally would use the word 'vegetarian' (somebody who does not eat meat).

b   Incompatible antonyms. It would be possible, however, to set up a context in which attention was limited to blue and red individuals: for example parliament under a strict two-party system, the football-supporting population of Liverpool, or Chinese chess (xiang qi). In such contexts they might be considered contradictory antonyms.

c   Incompatible antonyms, with the same reservation as in the previous answer.

d   As with 'vegetarian', usage of 'unmarried' varies. If you use it to include anybody is not currently married, then *unmarried* is a contradictory antonym of *married*. Many people, however, would not describe divorcees as 'unmarried'. For them the two words are incompatible antonyms.

4.17   a

P	Q	P → Q	(P → Q) & P	((P → Q) & P) → Q
t	t	t	t	t
t	f	f	f	t
f	t	t	f	t
f	f	t	f	t

Valid (guaranteed to be true)

b

P	Q	P → Q	~P	(P → Q) & ~P	~Q	((P → Q) & ~P) → ~Q
t	t	t	f	f	f	t
t	f	f	f	f	t	t
f	t	t	t	t	f	f
f	f	t	t	t	t	t

Invalid (not guaranteed to be true)

c

P	Q	P → Q	~Q	(P → Q) & ~Q	~P	((P → Q) & ~Q) → ~P
t	t	t	f	f	f	t
t	f	f	t	f	f	t
f	t	t	f	f	t	t
f	f	t	t	t	t	t

Valid

d

P	Q	P∨Q	~P	(P∨Q) & ~P	((P∨Q) & ~P) → Q
t	t	t	f	f	t
t	f	t	f	f	t
f	t	t	t	t	t
f	f	f	t	f	t

Valid

4.18 Many pairs of senses are incompatible, but are not felt as antonyms because they are not related (a). Thus the two must at least be hyponyms of the same concept. But this is not enough, because there may be too many hyponyms of the same concept for one of them to be felt as a unique 'opposite'; this happens with colour terms (c). Ideally two antonyms should have one contrasting property, like loud vs soft (b), or male vs female (d).

4.19 They are different because they contain a negation. If something is outside the larger set, then it must be outside the subset (denoted by the hyponym). Note that words like *forbidden* act like negatives – they contain an 'implicit negation'.

5.11 a Half of. twice(12, 6); half_of(6, 12)
 b Smaller than. bigger_than(tokyo, london); smaller_than (london, tokyo)
 c Teacher of. student_of(chomsky, harris); teacher_of (harris, chomsky)
 d Precede (or: be succeeded by). succeed(elizabeth, mary); precede(mary, elizabeth) or succeeded_by(mary, elizabeth)
 e Above. below(belgrade, vienna); above(vienna, belgrade)

**CHAPTER 5
Meaning
relations (2)**

5.12 buy(antonio, the_gun, don_marino)
sell(don_marino, the_gun, antonio)
cost(the_gun, antonio, $1000)
fetch(the_gun, don_marino, $1,000)

CHAPTER 6
Things and
events

6.4   normally mass (piece, lump)
         countable
         mass (piece, item)
         mass (no obvious measure word)
         as an animal skipping around, countable; as food on a plate,
            mass (piece, portion, joint)
         mass (spoonful, lump, kilo)
         as a metal, mass (piece, pig, ton); as a device for ironing, count-
            able
         mass (grain, bowl)
         mass (pint, bottle) – but like many foodstuffs it can be used
            countably when ordering ('two beers please').
         mass (bar, piece) – but countable when made into individual
            chocolates
         in English treated as a mass noun (piece)

6.5   They are interpreted as different *kinds* of the substance in question.

6.9   a   The plane is on the ground, then in the air.
         b   The room is untidy, then tidy.
         c   There is no fire, then there is one.
         d   Toad is not at the party, then he is at the party.
         e   People can see him, then they can't.

We know very little about the manner of change. We may imagine
a characteristic way of taking off, tidying a room, etc. But we supply
these details ourselves (or helped by the accompanying noun, like
'aeroplane'). We might assume that lighting a fire involves striking
a match, or that disappearing involves moving, but they can equally
well be done by magic for all the verbs tell us.

6.10 a   strode, shuffled, marched, goose-stepped, hobbled, lurched
             (information about the kind of movement, and inciden-
             tally about the people walking)
         b   strangle, drown, hang, guillotine (information about the
             manner and instrument used if any)
         c   begged, ordered, urged (manner of asking, reflecting the
             character or relationship between the two)
         d   shouted, whispered, mumbled (manner of speaking)
         e   beating, striking, hammering, stabbing, knifing, clubbing
             (information about the movement involved and in some
             cases about the instrument used)

In all these cases, the hyponym chosen does not have any significant effect on the result of the action.

6.11 Sentences a, b and d. Note the difference between a, which has it, and e, which doesn't.

6.13 Yes. The same sentences (a, b and d) have this property.

6.15 In sentences a and c, where the noun is a mass noun or a simple plural, the event is atelic. In b or d where it is countable, the event is telic.

6.16 They are telic, and in each case it is the change of state that is reversed. If any detail is given (or imagined) about the activity itself (tie, embark), it is not this characteristic activity (fiddling with shoelaces or walking) that is changed, but its result.

6.17 In the first pair of sentences (which contain activities) the action is repeated. In the second pair (which are changes of state each of which reverses the other), it implies that one was the 'original' state. (Note that 'again' is stressed in the first case, unstressed in the second.)

6.18 a   atelic; telic (destination); atelic (repeated action); telic (fixed period of time)
  b   the first strictly describes an instantaneous action – normally interpreted as repeated, which is an atelic activity; telic; atelic; telic
  c   atelic; telic ('to sleep' adds a result, or change of state); atelic; telic

---

6.19 The truth conditions change only in the case of the third sentence. This describes telic events, which seems to have the consequence that the actions are evaluated at different times (the first one is completed before the second one is evaluated). Note though that this does not apply to the fourth sentence, where the endpoints of the actions are not described (they are effectively 'invisible').

7.7 A = set of planes, B = set of entities which contain fuel

  a   A is a subset of B
  b   The intersection of A and B (A ∩ B) contains four individuals.
  c   A is a subset of B *and* A ∩ B contains four individuals.
  d   A and B are disjoint (no intersection).

CHAPTER 7
Quantifiers (1)

e   A contains at least one individual which is not in B (it is in A – B).

f   There is only one individual in A – B.

g   A ∩ B contains more individuals than A – B.

7.17   Only a and d have this property. It makes sense to talk about a set of honest entities (or people) and a set of green entities. 'Big' is a comparative term – a big mouse is not really a big entity. Similarly a good burglar is not, as such, a good entity (or person). As for 'former', it does not refer to a set of former entities, but simply to a relation that no longer holds.

7.18   a   the set of objects in London
b   the set of entities who wear bikinis
c   the set of entities who snore
d   the set of pieces composed by Mozart
e   the complement of the set of smokers

7.19   a   (examples) – the set of entities which breathe, the set of entities which eat. The set of people is a subset of all such sets.

b   'Somebody' denotes those sets which have a non-empty intersection with the set of people. (Example: the set of entities which swim.) 'Nobody' denotes those sets with an *empty* intersection with the set of people. (Example: the set of entities with four legs.)

c   'Nobody' denotes those sets with no intersection with the set of people. 'Nothing' denotes those sets with no intersection with the set of things.

7.20   In each case, the first is a subset of the second.

a   The first sentence entails the second. (If the set of sportspeople is a subset of the first, it must be a subset of the second.)

b   The first sentence entails the second.

c   The second sentence entails the first. (If a set does not intersect the larger set, it will not intersect the smaller.)

d   Assuming 'five' means *exactly five* (rather than *at least five*), neither sentence entails the other.

e   The second entails the first. Whatever number we take as being *few*, if there are few countries in the second set then there will be at least as few countries in the first set.

7.21 'Any' is appropriate with those quantifiers with which, in the previous exercise, the second sentence entailed the first (i.e. if its scope denotes a particular set then the sentence holds for all subsets of that set).

8.6 a   ∀x happy(x)
  b   ∃x snore(x)
  c   ~∃x sing(x)
  d   ~∃x like(x. harry)
  e   ∀x know(maninder, x)

CHAPTER 8
Quantifiers (2)

8.7 a   Somebody is clever.
  b   Everybody is asleep.
  c   Nobody knows Bill.
  d   Fagin killed somebody.
  e   Nobody forgets Risa.

8.9 a   ∀x, dog(x), smelly(x)
  b   ∃x, politician(x), honest(x)
  c   ∀x, child(x), love(x, mary)
  d   ~∃x, train(x), late(x)
  e   ∃x, animal(x), like(john, x)

8.14 a   ∀x (dog(x) → smelly(x))
  b   ∃x (politician(x) & honest(x))
  c   ∀x (child(x) → love(x, mary))
  d   ~∃x (train(x) & late(x))
      OR: ∀x ~(train(x) & late(x))
  e   ∃x (animal(x) & like(john, x))

8.15 a   Some Skodas work.
  b   All cities are dirty.
  c   No professors smile.
  d   All students know Mary.
  e   John reads no newspaper. (John doesn't read any newspaper)

8.17 a   ∀x ((city(x) & crowded(x)) → dangerous(x))
  b   ∃x ((student(x) & intelligent(x)) & rich(x))
  c   ~∃x ((woman(x) & beautiful(x)) & like(x, john))
  d   ~∃x ((politician(x) & honest(x)) & businessman(x))
  e   ∀x ((book(x) & useful(x)) → interesting(x))

Note that in b, c and d the inner set of brackets isn't really necessary, because ((P & Q) & R) is the same as (P & (Q & R)).

8.18   a $\forall x$ ((student(x) & know(x, john)) $\rightarrow$ know(x, mary))
          b $\sim\exists x$ ((student(x) & like(x, john)) & like(x, mary))
          c $\exists x$ ((tourist(x) & visit(x, london)) & rich(x))
          d $\forall x$ ((dish(x) & cook(maria, x)) $\rightarrow$ delicious (x))
          e $\exists x$ ((student(x) & drink(x, tequila)) & dance(x))

8.19   If you don't use the right connective with the right quantifier, then you get a perfectly good formula but it doesn't have the required meaning.

          a   This would mean that every object in the universe is both an Australian and a sportsperson.
          b   This would mean that for some object, if it is an Australian then it is also a sportsperson. But it doesn't assert that there are any such Australians.

8.20   a $\sim\exists x \sim$(australian(x) $\rightarrow$ sportsperson(x))
              There is no *x* which is in the set of *australians* but outside the set of *sportspeople*
          b $\sim\forall x \sim$(australian(x) & sportsperson(x))
              It is not the case that wherever you put an *x* it cannot be inside both the set of *australians* and the set of *sportspeople*

CHAPTER 9
Argument
structure

9.1   a   of a child
         b   probably of the person being addressed
         c   most importantly, of the person with the gun
         d   of the goods in question
         e   of the speaker's brain

9.3   In each case the theme and reference point occur in that order. The second sentences are odd because the reference point is expected to be a larger or more fixed object than the theme.

9.5   a   Sentences 1, 3, 4 and 7.
         b   The same. In general, if a path includes its endpoint the corresponding event will include an endpoint.

9.6 enter – into; approach – towards; reach – to; leave – out of, from
(All except 'approach' describe telic events.)

9.8 a devourer, thing devoured (both obligatory)
b eater, thing eaten (latter optional)
c clearer, surface cleared, things removed (last optional)
d clearer, things removed, place where they are removed from (last optional)
e giver, recipient, thing handed over (all obligatory)
f buyer, beneficiary, thing bought (beneficiary optional)

9.10 a Subject: 'Mary', Object: 'her pizza'. The *eater* role is assigned to *mary*, and the *eaten* role to *mary's_pizza*.
b (ditto)
c Subject: 'Sarah', Object: 'the table'. The *clearer* role is assigned to *sarah* and the *space_cleared* role to *the_table*.
d Subject: 'Sarah', Object: 'the plates'. The *clearer* role is again assigned to *sarah*, while the *object_removed* role is assigned to *the_plates*.

9.11 a Subject: 'Maria', Object: 'Angelica'.
b Subject: 'the students', Object: 'the pro-director'.
c Subject: 'the hedgehog', Object: 'the farmer'.

In all cases the referent of the subject is understood as doing something to that of the object. This is particularly striking in the last example, where farmers are more likely to do something to hedgehogs than the other way round.

9.12 The direct objects are all affected except in b and e. Although in these two they *may* be affected (by embarassment or by letting things go to his head), this is not specified by the verb. This is shown by the fact that the following are not contradictory:

a The builders saw Rachel walking down the road, but she didn't notice them.
b Many people admire Napoleon, but he is not aware of it.

9.14 bring / come; take / go; kill / die; drop / fall

9.17 1 (a) Theme: *pesticide*; Object: 'pesticide'
(b) Theme: *pesticide*; Object: 'the fields'

2   (a)   Theme: *vodka and tabasco*; Object: 'vodka and tabasco'

(b)   Theme: *vodka and tabasco*; Object: 'the tomatoes'

The first sentence of each pair is more natural if only a little of the substances has been used. The greater the effect on the fields or the tomatoes, the more likely they are to be expressed as the **object**.

9.18   'Pour' describes the manner of movement of a liquid, it cannot be construed as specifying a change of state in some background object like a container. By contrast 'fill' *must* specify the state of some container.

CHAPTER 10
Appendices

10.1   a $\emptyset$, {a}, {b}, {c}, {a, b}, {a, c}, {b, c}, {a, b, c}

b $\emptyset$, {a}, {{b, c}}, {a, {b, c}}

c $\emptyset$, {a}

d $\emptyset$, {a}, {b}, {$\emptyset$}, {c}, {a, b}. {a, $\emptyset$}, {a, c}, {b, $\emptyset$}, {b, c}, {$\emptyset$, c}, {a, b, $\emptyset$}, {a, b, c}, {a, $\emptyset$, c}, {b, $\emptyset$, c}, {a, b, $\emptyset$, c}

10.2   a   A is a (proper) subset of B

b   A is a (proper) superset of B

c   No subset relation

10.4   (1) Not all statements can be straightforwardly assigned one of the two truth values – cf. Exercise 2.1 (and there are other reasons as well). Some theories get round this by making truth assignment a *partial* function.

(2) Some expressions are ambiguous (and therefore do not have a unique value). Even a simple name like 'John' can easily refer to more than one individual.

10.3   LIST OF TECHNICAL TERMS

Numbers in brackets refer to chapters.

activity A situation where something is happening but not necessarily producing any overall change. (6)

antonym (of X) A word whose sense is the opposite of that of X. (4)

argument That part of a statement which describes one of the entities of which something (the **predicate**) is claimed to be true. (3)

atelic See **telic**. (6)

atomic Treated as if it cannot be broken down and analysed further. (3)

connective A symbol which joins two statements into a composite statement. (2)

construe (X) To interpret an expression X in a particular way, often a slightly unusual or forced way. (6)

contradiction A pair of statements which are opposites, in the sense that one must be false if the other is true and vice versa. (4)

converse (of X) A two-place **relation** which holds of the same entities as X but with the order of arguments reversed. (3, 10.1)

default Something which is assumed provisionally in the absence of any evidence to the contrary. (5)

denotation (of X) All the entities which can be described by an expression X. (1)

eventive Describing an event, a situation in which something happens. (6)

existential (quantifier) Used (with a statement) to mean that the statement is true of *some* entity of those under consideration. (In other words, that 'there is some entity' of which the statement is true.) (8)

function A two-place **relation** which pairs every entity in one set (the **domain**) with exactly one entity in another set (the **range**). (10.1)

homonym (of X) A word with the same form as X but different sense. (1)

hyponym (of X) A word sense which means a kind or subtype of X. (4)

implication (i) A relation between two statements such that if the first is true, the second must also be true. (ii) A connective whose truth tables are given on page 24. The first of these uses is also known as 'entailment', while the second is sometimes called 'material implication'. (4)

inheritance If a type of object has certain properties, then any subtype will (normally) also have these properties (along with others). For example, if being a dog involves having four legs then being a particular kind of dog (e.g. an alsatian) involves having four legs as well. (5)

incompatibility The relationship between two statements which cannot both be true. (4)

instance (of X) An object which is an example or specimen of X. (See **token**.) (9)

lexical semantics The study of word meaning. (1)

logic Can be thought of as the use of an artificial language or notation to bring out clearly whatever patterns or relations are regarded as significant (especially anything that contributes to the truth or falsity of expressions). The logical language introduced in this book involves predicates, arguments, connectives, quantifiers and variables. (1)

negation As used here, if a statement is true then its negation is false and vice versa. (2)

object As a syntactic term, the expression which is required to come after certain verbs. (9)

paraphrase (of X) An expression with the same meaning as X. (4)

pragmatics The study of how the meaning of an expression is affected by the context in which it is used. (1)

predicate That part of a statement which describes what is being claimed to be true of some entity or entities (the latter being its **arguments**). (3)

property Something which is true (or false) of a single entity. For example being green, being drunk, or snoring. (3)

prototype A typical example of a particular type of object – the example that people would naturally think of first. For example a prototypical pet would be a dog or cat rather than a crocodile. (5)

quantifier Used to make general statements about whole classes of entities rather than statements which are only true of a particular entity. For example 'all cities are dirty' (or for that matter 'no cities are dirty') involve quantifiers, whereas 'London is dirty' only conveys information about a particular entity. (7, 8)

reference (of X) The entity (or entities) picked out by an expression X on a particular occasion of utterance. (Cp. **sense**.) (1)

relation Something which is true (or false) of a pair of entities, or more. For example loving, or being bigger than, is true or false of pairs of entities; giving or buying are examples involving more than two entities at a time. (Something which is true of only one entity at a time is more normally known as a **property**.) (3, 10.1)

restriction The first of two sets related by a quantifier. It is normally specified by a noun (or similar expression) which accompanies the quantifier (e.g. some *snakes*). (7)

role The part played by an entity in a situation. A situation may require several entities, each having a different role. For example, you can't have a murder situation without a murderer and a victim. (3)

scope One of the sets related by a quantifier – specifically, the set denoted by the main **predicate** of the sentence (e.g. some snakes *bite*). (7)

semantic network A diagram representing relations between word meanings, particularly **hyponyms**. (5)

sense (of X) The meaning of a word X as opposed to its form. To be distinguished from word forms: one word form may have many senses, and several word forms may have one or more senses in common. Also to be distinguished from **reference**, which describes the entities in the world which instantiate it. For example, the sense of 'red' would be the concept of redness rather than any red *things*. (1)

subject As a syntactic term, the expression which is required to come before a predicate in order to make a complete sentence (e.g. *your mother* phoned). (9)

subset (of X) A set which contains only objects which are also in the set X. (10.1)

stative Describing a state, a situation in which nothing significant is happening. (6)

synonym of X A word form which shares at least one sense with X. (1)

telic An event which has a natural point where you can say that it is completed. (Opposite: **atelic**.) (6)

theme As used here: an entity whose location or state is being described. (9)

token (vs type) A particular instance or specimen of some **type**. (1)

truth-conditional semantics The study of sentence meaning attaching central importance to **truth conditions**. (1)

truth conditions The state of affairs which must hold for a statement to be true. (2)

truth values The possible verdicts on the truth of a sentence. Traditionally there are just two of them: *true* and *false*. (2)

type (vs token) A group of objects (**tokens**) which may be different but are judged to be 'the same' in all relevant respects. (1)

universal (quantifier) Used (with a statement) to mean that the statement is true of *all* entities under consideration. (8)

valid A logical argument (in fact any statement, such as $P \lor \sim P$) which is guaranteed to work out as *true*. (4)

variable A symbol which can stand for any entity. (It must stand for the same entity each time it occurs in a formula.) (8)

10.4 FURTHER READING

(References are to the Bibliography on pages 91–2.)

This book is a very basic introduction, and I have tried not to make it either very technical or very controversial. A useful next step would be to read one of the many general introductions to semantics available. Probably the most thorough and authoritative of these (at a basic level) is [14]. As a more advanced level, I recommend [10]; other popular resources are [15] and [1]. Much of this book has been concerned with constructing 'models' of the world using sets and relations. In most truth-conditional approaches this idea is taken seriously, and developed using mathematical 'model theory' – see [5] and [3]. These approaches can look a bit daunting, but the underlying ideas are largely those which you have begun to explore in this book. Formalization, properly used, is just a way of making ideas precise and stating them economically.

For serious work in semantics you will need some knowledge of certain areas of logic and mathematics. The best introductions to the use of these in linguistics are perhaps [5] or [16] respectively. A classic general introduction to logic is [6].

In Chapter 2 and subsequently the metaphor of 'windows' was used to introduce what I occasionally referred to (in a non-technical way) as 'possible worlds'. This idea has been developed by logicians as a subject in its own right, with a prolific literature. [5] includes a good introduction. For the full works, the classic textbook is [8].

Probably the most popular attempt to apply logic to semantics involves first order logic, and this is normally taught as standard. The alternative approach based on sets introduced in Chapter 7 is based on Generalized Quantifier Theory. This is not normally taught to beginners, but the ideas presented here seem to be quite intuitive, and there are some reasons to regard it as more useful for natural language. There are good sections on both approaches in [5] and [3], though they are not easy reading for beginners.

For lexical semantics, [7] offers a good introduction. [4] goes into more detail. You can read more about the idea of **prototypes** in [19]. For argument structure there are no obvious introductory texts, but the approach taken here is based on the work of Jackendoff, Pinker, and Levin and Rappaport (e.g. [9, 18, 12]). These works are not introductory, but they will probably not be found too inaccessible.

There is also an introduction to pragmatics in this series [17]. Another introductory book which I recommend (based on Relevance Theory) is [2]. The standard textbook is probably [13].

NOTE

1   A relation which is like a function from A to B except that it does not give a value for all members of A is called a partial function.

BIBLIOGRAPHY

[1] Allwood, J., L–G. Andersson and O. Dahl, *Logic in Linguistics*. Cambridge University Press, Cambridge, 1977.

[2] Blakemore, D., *Understanding Utterances*. Blackwell, Oxford, 1992.

[3] Chierchia, G. and S. McConnell-Ginet, *Meaning and Grammar*. MIT Press, Cambridge, Mass., 1990.

[4] Cruse, D., *Lexical Semantics*. Cambridge University Press, Cambridge, 1986.

[5] Gamut, L.T.F., *Logic, Language and Meaning*. 2 vols. University of Chicago Press, Chicago, 1991.

[6] Hodges, W., *Logic*. Penguin, London, 1977.

[7] Hudson, R., *Word Meaning*. Routledge, London, 1985.

[8] Hughes, G. and M. Cresswell, *A New Introduction to Modal Logic*. Routledge, London, 1995.

[9] Jackendoff, R., 'Semantics and Cognition'. In Lappin (1996), pp. 539–59.

[10] Kempson, R., *Semantic Theory*. Cambridge University Press, Cambridge, 1977.

[11] Lappin, S. (ed.), *Handbook of Contemporary Semantic Theory*. Blackwell, Oxford, 1996.

[12] Levin, B. and M. Rappaport Hovav, 'Lexical Semantics'. In Lappin (1996), pp. 487–507.

[13] Levinson, S., *Pragmatics*. Cambridge University Press, Cambridge, 1983.

[14] Lyons, J., *Linguistic Semantics*. Cambridge University Press, Cambridge, 1995.

[15] MacCawley, J., *Everything That Linguists Have Always Wanted To Know About Logic But Were Ashamed To Ask*. Blackwell, Oxford, 1981 (2nd edn, 1993).

[16] Partee, B., A. ter Meulen and R. Wall, *Mathematical Methods in Linguistics*. Kluwer, Dordrecht, 1990.

[17] Peccei, J., *Pragmatics*. Routledge, London, 1999.

[18] Pinker, S., *Learnability and Cognition: The Acquisition of Argument Structure*. MIT Press, Cambridge, Mass., 1989.

[19] Taylor, J., *Linguistic Categorization: Prototypes in Linguistic Theory*. Oxford University Press, Oxford, 2nd edn, 1995.